*Acts***29**

Blueprint
For the *House*
the
of
Prayer

Acts **29**

Blueprint
For
the *House*
*P*rayer
of

Dr. Terry Teykl

Prayer Point Press

Blueprint for the House of Prayer
Acts 29: Engaging Your City through Strategic Prayer
Copyright © 1997 Dr. Terry Teykl
Published by Prayer Point Press
Edited by Lynn Ponder
Cover Design: Jan Goff

First Edition, August 1997

ISBN: 1-57892-043-4
Printed in the United States of America

Prayer Point Press
2100 N. Carrolton Dr.
Muncie, Indiana 47304

Phone: (765) 759-0215
To order, call toll-free: (888) 656-6067

Dedication

This workbook is dedicated to Randy Wimpee,
my worship leader for sixteen years and my friend for life,
who taught me how to inspire unity through praise.

The one concern of the devil is to keep Christians from praying.
He fears nothing from prayerless studies, prayerless work, and prayerless religion.
He laughs at our toil, mocks at our wisdom, but trembles when we pray.
-Samuel Chadwick

Table of Contents

Study Questions at the end of each Unit.
Study Questions and Prayer Applications at the end of each Prayer Model.

Preface

It is called "Habitat for Humanity"—an organization committed to the idea that everyone deserves to have a home. All over America volunteers donate time, skill and labor to build houses for families in need. What a beautiful gesture of hope for society; a nostalgic reminder of an earlier time when communities were tied together by something more than just a sewer line.

But there is another kind of house that is being built in city after city. Churches, too, are organizing volunteers and building houses so that the Spirit of God can move in. They are inviting God to dwell in their cities, because where the life of God flows, good things happen: people come to Christ, relationships are healed, crime rates drop, churches are blessed. They are making a place for God in their neighborhoods, schools, and businesses. They are making provision for the Spirit to reside with them and make His presence known in their town. I call this movement "habitat for divinity," and when a church raises up a "habitat for divinity," the standard of spiritual living around it improves because the power of God is present.

Jesus said, "My house shall be called a house of prayer (Matt. 21:13)," and when we pray, He will come and dwell. The "habitat for divinity" is a house of prayer, built on a foundation of total dependence on Him and closed in by walls of faith. To construct it is a way of life—a life lived in intimacy with God, a life of knowing God as savior, healer and redeemer of lives and cities. It is not a home meant to confine God to live within the four walls of the church, but rather it is a place from which His Spirit moves and works in the area around it. A thriving house of prayer will impact individual lives, neighborhoods and cities; it will yield unity, mercy and salvation; and it will be an oasis of hope and reconciliation.

However, it is not enough to just talk about building a house of prayer. It is not even enough to have all of the raw materials in your possession. No one can live in a vision and a pile of bricks. If you want to build a house, you must have a blueprint. No structure, regardless of its size or architectural style, was ever constructed without one. Blueprints dictate every line and angle. For those who are trained to read them, they contain every piece of essential information that is needed to build the house. They insure that not only will the finished product look exactly like the builder intended for it to, but also that it will be structurally sound.

After studying the prayer lives of hundreds of churches, I am convinced that the house of prayer also starts with a blueprint. I have also determined that, for some reason, many churches try to raise up prayer with little or no planning at all. Unlike most other ministries, prayer seems to be one that we leave up to chance, just hoping that our members know what to do and are doing it. In many cases prayer efforts are haphazard, inconsistent, and unconnected. They follow no master plan because there is no master plan, and the result more closely resembles a shanty than a well-designed mansion.

The purpose of this workbook is to provide you with a set of blueprints from which to build your house of prayer. It is a draft of the principles and designs that you can consult as you go through the building process. It will help you determine the cost of building, both to be prayed and payed, and it will stimulate your thinking as you pick and choose which combination of strategies you will implement.

Since every house of prayer will be different, listen to the Holy Spirit for direction, because He is the Architect. He wants to design His home in your church so that He can manifest Himself in your city just as He did in the book of Acts. As you begin to pray, He will stir in you a passion for the lost, a vision for unity, and a fresh love of the Father. May you be blessed as you seek to know Him and make Him known in your city.

Notes to Instructors

1. This workbook is designed to be taught in any type of small group setting such as a Sunday school class, cell group or Bible study. It can also be used for individual study. The lessons are not numbered because it is expected that the instructor will adapt the material for the duration of the course, which may vary from just a few weeks to an entire semester.

2. This workbook contains 16 sets of study questions, at the end of Units 1 through 6 and following each of the ten Acts 29 Prayer Models. Because these sections vary in length, the instructor may wish to combine sections if necessary. It might also be helpful for the instructor to consult with the pastor and prayer leaders about which Prayer Models to emphasize, since different churches are better equipped to implement some than others.

3. In addition to study questions, each of the ten Acts 29 Prayer Models is followed by a Prayer Application. These are short, daily prayer exercises that allow the reader to incorporate some aspects of the Prayer Model into their personal prayer time. They can be used in conjunction with the lessons taught from the Prayer Models, or at any other time during the course. The instructor might suggest that the readers make short notes as they pray through these Applications so that these pages can function like a personal prayer journal.

4. Note that on many of the lessons, resources are listed for additional information. Since this workbook is intended to be an overview of prayer basics and strategies, it is recommended that the instructor be familiar with the resources pertaining to the Models he or she chooses to emphasize.

Introduction

For the Son of Man came to seek and save what was lost.
Luke 19:10

Small and white, it looked no different than all the other houses that lined the gang-ridden streets in the heart of Bryan, Texas. But for some reason, it beckoned the three women who drove that neighborhood praying every Saturday morning. They would sometimes stop their car across the street and say a special prayer for the people living there, totally unaware of the magnanimous plan of God in which they were playing a key part.

The three women—a housewife, a teacher and a business woman—had been doing this "drive-by" praying every weekend for several months. They were faithful, even tenacious. It was a crazy idea that God had inspired in two of the women as they prayed in the prayer room at our church. When they first started, they would drive around the entire city, circling it in prayer. Then, as they felt led, they began identifying specific places in the city—high crime areas, bars, pornography houses, gang hang-outs—and they would drive by these places, inviting the Holy Spirit to come and telling Satan he had to go. They had no idea that their prayers would eventually rewrite the future of a young drug dealer named J. J. Ramirez.

J. J. was, at that time, identified by the Bryan police department as one of the leading drug dealers in the city. His was living life at the brink of destruction, ensnared by drugs, alcohol, failed relationships, lost jobs, gangs, fights and weapons. He was tough. The streets demanded it. In the eyes of the local authorities, he was a good-for-nothing criminal. But in the eyes of God, he was a perfect candidate for evangelist!

In an intricately woven set of family circumstances, amidst the barrage of prayers of three women he did not even know existed, J. J. found himself at a Carman concert, where he felt the powerful love of God for the first time in his life. He gave his heart to Jesus that night, and to say the least, his life was dramatically changed.

With the same intensity that he once pushed drugs, he began pushing Jesus and the life-changing power of the blood. His living room filled up every evening with young boys from the gangs who would sit and clean their weapons while they listened to him preach the Gospel that he had just discovered. They respected him, and what he lacked in "religious knowledge," he made up for in sincerity. God had hand-picked J. J. to minister in places that no one else could go.

His ministry grew as quickly as his own spiritual understanding. Our church took him in and began supporting him and providing him with resources when he needed them. He handed out Bibles from the trunk of his car. He pitched a tent in the street for three nights and saw 78 young people, many from rival gangs, come to Christ and be baptized!

Resource:
Fresh Encounter
Henry Blackaby, Claude King

10

Even at our church, we began baptizing one or two gang members each Sunday because J. J. would bring them to the service.

Then something so extraordinary happened that it could only be explained by the work of the Holy Spirit. A local high school principal who had heard about J. J.'s work in the streets invited him to speak to his entire student body in an assembly. Knowing the religious tightrope that public schools walk, J. J. reluctantly told the principal that he would love to speak, but that he had only one message—Jesus. He said if he could not preach Jesus, then he really would have nothing to say. That high school principal looked back at J. J., undaunted by his long ponytail and earring, and said, "Go for it! Say anything you like. These kids need what you have."

At the end of that first school assembly, in a packed-out gymnasium, over half of the student body stood to profess faith in Jesus Christ! The response to J. J.'s street wise language and simple message of salvation was unprecedented. Within one week, more invitations to area public schools began pouring in, and almost overnight, J. J. was launched out as an evangelist in territory that traditionally had been more sealed off than some communist countries.

Today, J. J. is still in the heart of Bryan running "Save Our Streets" Ministry (S.O.S.). He holds summer camp programs, Bible studies and gang reconciliation services, and he continues to reach hundreds of kids, many of whom are involved in gangs, drugs and violence. In addition, one of the unexpected benefits of J. J.'s ministry has been the unity of purpose that it has given to the churches of the city. Over fifty of them currently support S.O.S. Ministry, making them partners in this exciting outreach.

I believe there is a "J. J." in every city in America. They are chosen of God and anointed for a special purpose. But unless we are willing to pray the price, we may never see them come forth. God works through the prayers of His people, and it is our responsibility and our privilege to be obedient in prayer in behalf of those in our cities who need desperately to know Him.

Imagine this...

A retired D. C. police officer, whose son was killed in the streets, showed such forgiveness for his son's killer that he stood at the trial set to convict the boy and pled with the jury for leniency. When the boy got out of prison, he went to live with the officer and his wife who raised him as their own son.

It is impossible to lose your footing while on your knees.
-Anonymous

Introduction

A City-Wide Perspective

As remarkable as J. J.'s story is, it is even more amazing that stories like this one are happening all over the country. We are in the middle of one of the greatest prayer surges in history, and many are seeing unprecedented results. Jesus said, "...open your eyes and look at the fields! They are ripe for harvest" (John 4:35). That statement has never been more true, and today, it is taking on a city-wide perspective.

In Fayetteville, North Carolina, as Christians from several churches have banded together to prayerwalk around areas of violent crime, the overall crime rate in that city has dropped by 50 percent! In Muncie, Indiana, several leaders from different churches developed a prayer group which included the mayor. When the city ran out of funding for the local relief shelters, they voted to allow the churches to take over that outreach. Now, when people visit one of the shelters in search of food, clothing or medical help, they receive the good news of the Gospel as well. In Ventura, California, one Episcopal congregation "fasted" going to church for one month. On Sunday mornings, instead of gathering for worship, they strategically covered their neighborhoods, hanging a written prayer of blessing on every door in the entire city. When they resumed their regular church services, instead of finding decreased attendance, which some had told them was inevitable, they found over 700 new faces in their pews!

Just as world evangelization aimed at hundreds of identified unreached people's groups is being organized and strategized like never before in history, city-wide evangelism is also emerging as the challenge for local churches of every size and flavor. As denominational walls are crumbling and more and more cooperation is being fostered within the true body of Christ, the scope of evangelistic outreach has shifted to encompass entire cities, counties, and even states. Many churches are turning their focus outward, finding creative ways to take Jesus beyond the four walls of their buildings and out into neighborhoods, schools, businesses, medical facilities, law enforcement departments, city government offices, jails, nursing homes—even night clubs and bars.

The Challenge

If it is happening everywhere else, why not in your city, town or community? God really desires to advance His Kingdom where you live, and you are His foot soldier. He has a plan and a purpose for every community, and He has chosen us—His church—as the mechanism through which to accomplish it. That means that God will only be creative to the degree that we are willing to let go of our man-serving tradi-

Resources:

Primary Purpose
Ted Haggard

That None Should Perish
Ed Silvoso

tions and imagine with Him; He will only display His power to the degree that we are willing to be bold for Him; and He will only answer prayers that we have faith enough to pray.

The purpose of this manual is to engage you and your church in the purpose and energy of this exciting prayer evangelism movement. It is designed to aid you as individuals and as a corporate body in effectively reaching the lost in your city for Jesus. That is the primary purpose.

Before you begin, consider the following questions:

1. Jesus told us to go and make _____ of all people.
   A. conservatives
   B. charismatics
   C. _____ (your denomination)
   D. disciples
2. As a Christian, your goal should be to lift up the name of
   A. yourself
   B. your church
   C. your pastor
   D. Jesus
3. As a church, our motivation for reaching the lost should be
   A. to increase our attendance so that giving will increase
   B. to make our church the most popular church in town
   C. to impress our denominational leaders
   D. to answer God's desire that none should perish

It is critical that you understand that the objective of this manual is to motivate and equip you to reach pre-believers for Jesus. It is not about denominational facsimiles or evangelism awards. It is not about building your church, but rather building the Kingdom of God where you live. It is about salvation for every person, and the rule and reign of Jesus in your city.

> *Imagine this...*
>
> *Seventy churches in El Paso, Texas co-sponsored a free Bible distribution in a program called "The Year of the Bible." They rented several billboards in town and advertised with a phone number to call. Currently, between thirty and forty Bibles are being given away every day, and many of the recipients pray to receive Christ over the phone.*

It will take a citywide church to win the citywide war. Our separate, isolated efforts will not stop the flood of increasing evil in our cities if we, as Christ's Church, remain isolated from each other.

-Francis Frangipane

For Group Discussion

1. Is there a person in your town who, if converted, would be able to draw large numbers of unreached people to Christ?

2. What is our primary purpose?

3. On any given Sunday, what percentage of your city's population does <u>not</u> attend church?

4. What does your church do to reach the unchurched?

5. If you were to make yourself available to God, where might he send you in your city? Would you go?

In Closing: Pray for a passion to reach the unchurched.

As He...saw the city, he wept over it and said, "...you did not recognize the time of God's coming to you."
Luke 19:41, 44

Notes

He called you to this through our gospel, that you
might share in the glory of our Lord Jesus Christ.
II Thessalonians 2:14

Biblical Basis for Prayer

In the beginning, God gave the responsibility of rulership of the earth to Adam and Eve. But, as we all know, they fell. In order to redeem His original intent, God introduced a series of covenants, the last of which would be the New Covenant ratified by Jesus' death on the cross. Through covenant, all that God is, He committed to His people with His presence, guidance, provision and protection.

The benefits of the Covenant are realized and actualized through prayer, both personal and corporate. Therefore, prayer is an intimate and powerful relationship between God and His people. It is His vehicle by which He invades the world with His will, and it is His portal of blessing into our lives and cities (Matt. 21:21, Mark 11:23-24, I Thess. 5:17).

So why does prayer work? Understanding the dynamics of this covenant relationship will help us grasp the biblical basis for prayer.

1. Prayer access to the Old Testament Covenant was in the names of God.

> Jehovah - The Great I Am (Ex. 3:14)
> Jehovah Jireh - The Provider (Gen. 22:14)
> El Shaddai - The Lord God Almighty (Gen. 49:24-25)
> Adonai - Our Shield (Gen. 15:1-3)
> Jehovah Rophi - The Healer (Ex. 15:26)
> Jehovah M Kadesh - The Righteous One (Lev. 20:7-8)
> Jehovah Nissi - Our Banner (Ex. 17:15)

Prayer access to the New Testament Covenant is in one name: Jesus. That is why He said, "And I will do whatever you ask in my name, so that the Son may bring glory to the Father" (John 14:13).

2. The Covenant is based on God's word. God gave us His word, and it is good, trustworthy and not to be broken. Prayer in this covenant is based on the vocabulary and language of His word which is why Jesus said, "If you remain in me and my words remain in you, ask whatever you wish and it will be given you" (John 15:7).

> His word...
> ...is the word of promise (Deut. 26:16-19).
> ...generates faith (Rom 10:17).
> ...is His will (I John 5:14-15, Luke 19:3, Matt. 6:10).
> ...represents His power over doubt and fear (Heb. 4:12, Is. 55:10).
> ...puts us in agreement with God (Matt. 18:18-20, Acts 1:14).
> ...provides content, direction, scope and a variety of intercession, insights, and revelations (II Chron. 20, Eph. 3:14-21, Eph. 6).

Resources:

Prayer
Richard Foster

Praying with Power
C. Peter Wagner

3. The Covenant relationship is based on trust. That means that it is faith in God that drives prayer. We pray because we believe God is able and willing, and that He is perfect in His dealings with us.

4. The Holy Spirit is the co-sponsor of prayer in the human spirit. He is our helper (Rom. 8:26). As Jesus sits on the throne interceding for the Father's purpose to be fulfilled, He dispatches the Holy Spirit to pray in us, through us and by us. In turn, as we lift our hearts to God, we become His agents in the earth. The more we pray, the more we become molded and shaped to His heart.

5. The Holy Spirit comes on the scene in answer to prayer. All through Luke's account of Jesus' life, and in the book of Acts, we see a pattern of prayer inviting the Holy Spirit. For example, in Luke 3:21 we read, "When all the people were being baptized, Jesus was baptized too. And <u>as he was praying</u>, heaven was opened and the Holy Spirit descended upon him like a dove." Again in Luke 5:15-16, we see that Jesus often withdrew to pray, and that the power of the Lord (the Holy Spirit) was present for Him to heal the sick. There is a direct correspondence between prayer and the movement of the Holy Spirit.

The disciples experienced a similar relationship because when they prayed in Acts 1:14, the Holy Spirit fell upon them in Acts 2. The same thing happened in Acts 9:11 and 9:17, 10:9 and 10:44, 16:13 and 16:14, 16:16 and 16:18, 16:25 and 16:32-33. Over and over we see the principle at work—prayer invites the Holy Spirit.

"Blue Northers"

In Texas, when a cold air mass moves down from Canada, people sometimes refer to it as a "Blue Norther," and it makes its presence felt! You can feel the wind blow as the high pressure cold air rushes into the warmer area of lower pressure. The greater the difference in pressure between the high and the low, the greater the wind speed.

Prayer creates in us a kind of low pressure area as we bow in humility before the Lord. The "lower" we can become through prayer, the stronger the wind will be when the high pressure of the Spirit blows in. He will make His presence felt in our lives and in our cities.

- -

Because God is the living God,
he can hear;
because he is a loving God,
he will hear;
because he is our covenant God,
he has bound himself to hear.
-Charles Spurgeon

17

Biblical Basis for Prayer

The Holy Spirit is the real evangelist. We are only here to release Him to work. This is the drive shaft of covenant prayer evangelism, that when we pray, He works not only in us, but also in the non-believer to accomplish God's purpose.

The Holy Spirit's Work in Us

1. Compassion

To have a passion for evangelism is to care enough about the souls of those we meet that we will go to any length to see that they are secured for eternity. We reach out to people because we love, and we love because He first loved us. The first thing the Spirit does in us when we begin to pray is put the compassion of Jesus in our hearts for those who do not know Him, especially those who might be hurting, confused or unlovable.

2. Urgency

How easy it is to fall into the habit of conducting church business as usual—get the mail, answer the phone, conduct services, order new candles, get more mail, order new choir robes, conduct more services, and answer more calls. We can become so programmed that we totally lose sight of the meaning behind what we are doing. The result is that our end-of-the-year report looks just like the one before. We have passed the time as if "doing" church was our main objective.

God have mercy on us for just going through the motions! Our mission is one of eternal consequences and we must never lose sight of the gravity of it. As we pray, the Holy Spirit will continually renew our urgency to seek and save the lost.

3. Vision

Finally, as we pray, the Spirit gives us a vision for how to evangelize our city. He will plant a vision for prayer evangelism in anyone who will pray for the Great Commission and sit still long enough to hear His response. I meet people all over the country who are absolutely driven by a vision God has given them for their church or city. Individuals like the apostle Paul, Martin Luther and Billy Graham were all ordinary Christians who were not afraid to embrace God-sized vision and purpose.

The Holy Spirit's Work in Unbelievers

1. Convict and Convince

When we begin to ask God to give us the lost people in our cities, the Holy Spirit goes to work in every unbeliever to gently convict them of their sin and convince them of their need for God. Remember, He is

Resource:

I Believe in the Holy Spirit
Michael Green

the true Evangelist.

Although we can not literally see this work going on, it means the difference between success and failure in all of our evangelistic efforts. Jesus said, "No one can come to me unless he is drawn by the Father" (John 6:44), meaning that the gentle prodding of the Holy Spirit is what ushers a person into the Kingdom. When God brings together a Christian who is user-friendly and an unbeliever who has been wooed by the Holy Spirit, then evangelism happens almost effortlessly.

2. Tear Down Walls

In every city, there are unseen forces that can hinder people from receiving Christ or can cause them to resist the Gospel. For example, in some cities, racism and prejudice are so rampant between people groups that none of the churches can minister effectively. In other places, disunity among the believers plays havoc with evangelistic efforts. Sometimes there are spiritual forces that need to be disarmed in order for large numbers of people to come to Christ. The second thing the Holy Spirit begins to do when we pray is to tear down the walls of resistance in the city that are hindering the spread of our message.

3. Change the Spiritual Climate

Just as every city has a physical climate that affects the temperature, rainfall, humidity and so forth, they also have a spiritual climate that may determine the fertility for evangelism. Every city, big or small, has its own "feel"—the people are different, the attitudes are unique and the priorities may vary. To some degree, that uniqueness is related to the spiritual background and receptivity, making some places easier to witness in than others. As we pray, the Holy Spirit can move in the heavenly realm to affect that aspect of the climate that we can not even touch.

4. Bring People to Jesus

Finally, as we pray, we will see people drawn to Jesus because the Evangelist is at work. The more we come alive to Christ, the more we can offer a life in Christ to others. Jesus said, "...open your eyes and look at the fields! They are ripe for harvest" (John 4:35). The end result of prayer will be seeing people living in the fullness of Christ for the first time.

Imagine this...

One pastor identified two groups of 80 people in the phone directory. One group received prayer for 90 days, and the other did not. At the end of the prayer time, both groups were called for prayer requests. Of the 80 not prayed for, none shared any needs. Of the 80 who had received prayer, 79 openly asked for prayer and some even invited the callers over for coffee.

If Christians spent as much time praying as they do grumbling, they would soon have nothing to grumble about.
-Anonymous

1. Based on the idea of covenant, why does God answer prayer?

2. Why do you think the disciples were forbidden to speak in the name of Jesus?

3. Relate a time when it was evident to you that the Holy Spirit was at work as a result of prayer.

4. Do you feel that you have a passion for the lost? Why or why not?

5. Whose job is it to win the lost? As you review the seven works of the Holy Spirit, discuss why evangelism without prayer could be hazardous.

In Closing: Pray for more prayer in your life, your church and your city.

One of his disciples said to him, "Lord, teach us to pray."
Luke 11:1

Notes

Then the Lord said: "I am making a covenant with you. Before all your people I will do wonders never before done in any nation....   Exodus 34:10

Prayer Evangelism

If it is not apparent to you that our cities and towns are in trouble, then you must be living in a cave. Turn on the news or pick up a newspaper and you see the symptoms—hate crimes, random killings, illegal dealings, betrayal. It is almost as if, not far below the surface of humanity, there churns a volcano of anger, bitterness, hatred and jealousy, and at the slightest provocation, it erupts into violence.

And just how effective is the church today at halting this social decline? Not very, according to most sources. The sad reality is that on many fronts, the American Church is struggling just to exist. In the face of real life problems, our churches are anemic and turned in on themselves. C. Peter Wagner states that only 1% of the churches in America are currently growing by conversion growth, and that no county across the nation has shown a net growth in Christianity in the last two decades. Furthermore, in my own denominational conference, over 40% of the churches did not record one single profession of faith in all of 1996! That represents a lot of church services in which no one received Jesus.

So what is going on? With 242,000 churches in America, billions of dollars in combined assets, and a building of some kind on just about every corner, why are we not more effective in demonstrating the Gospel to a hurting society and bringing people into the Kingdom? I believe it is because we have committed a "great *o*mission."

The Great Divorce

In the days of the early church, when Paul, Silas, Timothy, Peter and others were spreading the news of Christ throughout all of Asia Minor, the practice of prayer and the work of evangelism were one and the same. Perhaps this was because the disciples had nothing else to rely on—no money, no buildings, no programs, no modern communications technology. Or it could be that they simply knew the power of prayer and understood why Jesus had spent so much time praying Himself. Regardless, they turned their world upside down with little more than the clothes on their back and the prayers on their lips.

Unfortunately, somewhere along the way, as the church developed and made great strides in organization and resources, prayer and evangelism grew apart and eventually separated, each going its own way. Prayer became listless; it had no list of the lost. It became visionless; it lost sight of those who were unsaved. It was lame; it could not even meet church members' needs. It was tame; it set no captives free. Prayer married itself off to self-serving attitudes and man-centered agendas.

Evangelism, on the other hand, was in trouble as well. It gave in

Resource:
A Time to Pray God's Way
Evelyn Christensen

to hard-sell tactics, marketing techniques and advertising schemes. It became programatic, turning out memorized presentations of a Gospel turned academic. It bought into methods and turned them into sales campaigns. When it could not produce converts, it settled for producing good attendance or starting a scouting troop. When it could not generate professions of faith, it was happy to just "get them in the building."

The two, once so imtimately bound together, have suffered and struggled along on their own. But the real victims are the children—lost children who need to be brought home. The ones who are suffering are the hundreds and thousands of pre-believers who are desperate for hope and salvation, and it is for their sake that we must bring prayer and evangelism back together.

A Match Made in Heaven

Prayer evangelism is by no means a new concept. In fact, the two were meant to be together from the start. The book of Acts chronicles example after example of how the two are intertwined. In fact, I think it is safe to say that one of the primary functions of prayer in the Kingdom of God is to bring people to the point of salvation.

Look at Acts 16. Verses 13 and 14 read, "On the Sabbath we went outside the city gate to the river, where we expected to find a place of prayer. We sat down and began to speak to the women who had gathered there. One of those listening was a woman named Lydia.... The Lord opened her heart to respond to Paul's message." In the next scene, we read, "Once when we were going to the place of prayer, we were met by a slave girl..." (v. 16). Several verses later, we find that the girl who was troubled is set free and evidently receives the Gospel. Verses 22 through 34 tell the story of how Paul and Silas made a prayer room out of their jail cell, and then shared Christ with the jailer. He asks them, "Sirs, what must I do to be saved?" "Believe in the Lord Jesus, and you will be saved—you and your household" (vs. 30-31), they replied. And the jailer and all his family were immediately baptized.

The Lord is not slow in keeping his promise. He is patient with you, not wanting anyone to perish, but everyone to come to repentance.   II Peter 3:9

The book of Acts is the story of things happening as the disciples were going to pray, while they were praying, and after they prayed. In just one chapter, three examples of prayer yielded three examples of evangelism. For the apostles in the early church, prayer evangelism was the very essence of life.

Prayer Evangelism

The good news about prayer and evangelism is that all over the world they are being reunited with unprecedented passion. Evangelistic prayer that targets the Great Commission is being organized all over the world with New Testament results. For example, the United Prayer Track has mobilized 36 million people to pray for one hundred gateway cities in unevangelized nations. Harvest Evangelism, founded by Ed Silvoso and fueled by his book *That None Should Perish*, has launched city-wide prayer evangelism strategies in hundreds of cities. Pray USA!, which is a prayer initiative of Mission America, launched thirty days of prayer and fasting in April of 1997 for our country to return to God. Houses of Prayer Everywhere is planting prayer cells in neighborhoods and workplaces all over the country praying for friends, neighbors and co-workers who need to know Jesus. We are seeing the best of prayer married to the best of evangelism for genuine results.

New Prayer

This new prayer evangelism surge has given rise to a new kind of prayer. Where once prayer tended to be focused inward, crisis-motivated and us-centered, it is now becoming visionary, outward and others-centered. Prayer is being catapulted outside the walls of our churches and into communities, states and nations. This new prayer has several distinguishing characteristics:

1. **It is driven by a Kingdom agenda.** It is no longer being fueled by man-centered programs and plans, but by compelling questions like, "What is God's vision for our church?" "What is His will?" "What would He have us do to reach the lost in our area?" It is about "Thy Kingdom come, Thy will be done."
2. **It is based on the assumption that we need the Holy Spirit** in order to affect our cities for God. While we may be able to do some good things with a lot of money and a good location, we can only do extraordinary, supernatural things, such as changing lives, through the power of the Holy Spirit.
3. **It is the fulfillment of John 17:23** which says, "May they be brought to complete unity to let the world know you sent me." It seeks unity in the body of Christ, and is the answer to Jesus' call for complete cooperation among believers.
4. **It is is both thriving on and producing a wide array of quality prayer materials.**
5. **It is a grass roots movement.** The players in the new prayer initiatives are housewives, businessmen and women, students

Resources:

Praying For You
Howard Tryon

Personal Prayer Evangelism
Terry Teykl

and skilled laborers. The new prayer movement is being carried not by a select group of spiritual giants or an elite class of intercessors, but by "ordinary" people who are willing to pray the price.

6. **It is the apex of all that we do**, not simply a parachute that we open as a last resort. It is our foundation which determines our course, and it saturates everything.

7. **It is a means to an end.** Rather than just doing prayer as another program, new prayer seeks to attach prayer in every manner to the Great Commission. It is only a vehicle through which we can accomplish the purposes of God.

Praying the Price

Establishing new prayer in your church and city is a process. It is not something you can do one day and not the next, nor is it a program that can be implemented or a recipe that can be followed. Rather, praying the price is a way of life. It is a mindset, or a paradigm, that governs every decision we make and every action we take. It calls us to get out of the driver's seat and let God be God. Here are eight keys that will help you establish an attitude of new prayer:

1. Build a solid, living theology of prayer.
2. Seek a vision for what God wants to do in your city.
3. Develop a plan to bring the vision to pass.
4. Establish visible leadership for prayer.
5. Become familiar with prayer resources.
6. Recruit people to pray.
7. Train people to pray strategically.
8. Turn plans into action.

I looked for a man among them who would build up the wall and stand before me in the gap on behalf of the land so I would not have to destroy it....
Ezekiel 22:30

For Group Discussion

1. Ed Silvoso says, " Prayer is evangelism." Do you agree or disagree?

2. What image comes to mind when you hear the word "evangelism"?

3. How would you describe the current relationship in your church between prayer and evangelism?

4. Where in your church could prayer be coupled with evangelism strategies that are already in place?

5. Do you know someone that has been turned off by "hard-sell" evangelism? What can you do to reverse their negative feelings?

In Closing: Pray for the healing of all who have been hurt or turned off by hard-sell evangelism.

...with your blood you purchased men for God from every tribe and language and people and nation.
Rev. 5:9

Guidelines for the Shield A Badge Participants

(A prayer ministry to Houston Police Officers)

1. Commitment for one year to pray daily for an officer.
2. The officer's name, badge number and agency will be all that is given to the intercessor.
3. Communications from the participant to the officer are to be limited to no more than four pieces of mail per year.
4. No efforts should be made to make personal contact.
5. No gifts are to be given to the officer.
6. The intercessor should enter the program with no ulterior motives or expectations.
7. You may use your name and address on correspondence, allowing the officer to respond if he or she desires.

Suggestions for Intercessors

1. Post the name of your officer where you will see it daily.
2. Ask for the Holy Spirit's guidance as you pray. Pray for protection, family safety, self-control, etc.
3. Include all uniformed peace officers in your prayers.
4. Pray as though the officer's life depends on your prayer.

Adapted from Shield A Badge Material, Second Baptist Church in Houston

Pray without ceasing.
I Thessalonians 5:17

Mobilizing to Pray

It would be silly to plunge into a discussion of corporate prayer without first examining our own personal prayer attitudes and habits. Although personal prayer is not the focus of this workbook, it is the essential foundation that undergirds any church or city-wide prayer ministry. Our own theology of prayer—we all have one whether we realize it or not—determines how we pray, how often we pray and what we expect when we pray. A church that desires to have strong prayer ministries must first invest in building the individual prayer lives of its members.

There can be no question that personal devotions are of critical importance to our spiritual lives. We see strong private prayer modeled in the disciples, the saints of the Old Testament such as Moses, Samuel, Elijah and Daniel, giants of the faith such as Wesley, Finney and Luther, and of course ultimately in Jesus Himself. Even the Son of God, who was one with the Father, prayed to know God, to know His will, to have power to do His will, and to have perseverance in His will. Jesus did not only practice prayer, He taught it. That is good news for those of us who feel unsure about our prayer lives because it means prayer can be learned! It is a discipline and skill that we can study, practice and improve.

Many good books and devotionals have been written that can enhance your time with God, but I would like to offer you three "P's" that I have learned over the years in the area of personal prayer: Preparation, Practical Tips and Principles.

Preparation

1. Invite the Holy Spirit. He is your helper in prayer and He will come when you humble yourself.
2. Take the name of Jesus. Praying in His name means that God hears your prayers based on who Jesus is, not who you are.
3. Trust that God hears you. Faith is an attitude of expectation and confidence. It pulls your thoughts and words into alignment with what God has already said.
4. Pray the Word of God. The Bible is the richest prayer resource you will ever find. Praying the scriptures means praying the answers, not the problems.

Practical Tips

1. Be simple. Prayer is a conversation with someone you love. You speak, then you listen.
2. Be specific. Do not be afraid to tell God exactly what you need.
3. Be spontaneous. Love relationships thrive on creativity.

Resources:

The Hour That Changes the World
Dick Eastman

Don't Just Stand There, Pray Something
Ronald Dunn

4. Be outspoken. Sometimes it is helpful to actually hear the words coming out of your mouth.
5. Be conversational. God is not limited to "King James" English.
6. Be in place. Having a special place for prayer helps set your time apart.
7. Be ready to write. If you are willing to be still and listen, God may give you an idea, thought or vision. Record it.
8. Be forgiving. Never go through your prayer time with anger, resentment or negative feelings in your spirit.
9. Be willing to change. Prayer is a crucible for personal growth and renewal.
10. Begin. Do not wait until you have cleaned up your life.

Principles

1. Praise - Starting your prayer time by worshipping God for who He is is not only proper protocol, it also moves our focus off of ourselves and onto the Father.
2. Waiting - Being still and quiet before the Lord is the hardest thing for most of us to do, but it is also the most rewarding. Give God a chance to talk.
3. Petitioning - Now you are ready to ask. God takes pleasure in meeting the needs of His children.
4. Thanksgiving - Thank Him for who He is and what He has already done in your life.
5. Appropriation - This means learning how to receive from God. Thank Him in advance for hearing and answering your request.
6. Action - Ask the Lord to show you what specific actions you might take that could bring about the answers to your own prayers.

Another aspect of prayer that many find helpful is journaling. Keeping a **prayer journal** offers several advantages:
1. It provides a means to record and reflect on the deeds of God.
2. It is a way to trace your own spiritual progress.
3. It gives you a place to record goals, prayer requests and answers.
5. It offers you a place to write out special prayers.
6. It helps you to remember important decisions, revelations and experiences.
7. It helps you to experiment with different kinds of prayer.
8. It gives you a place to keep track of verses of scripture that have special meaning to you.

Imagine this...

Esther Ilnisky of Esther Network International has raised up two million children to pray for world evangelization.

Intimacy could be defined as "In-to-me-you-see."
-Kay Teykl

Mobilizing to Pray

I have noticed a trend. As I have traveled around the country and visited many churches, I have concluded that in many ways our ministries are highly organized. However, when it comes to prayer, we often have no plan, no leadership, no goals, no recruitment efforts and no training. We just hope that people are praying and we hope they know what they are doing.

Ironically, prayer is the one ministry that Jesus wanted the church to carry out. He said that His house should be called a "house of prayer," not a house of preaching, singing or board meetings. He knew that in order for the church to fulfill its mission, it would have to be dependent on, submersed in and fueled by prayer. He knew that we could do nothing except through prayer—inviting the Holy Spirit to come and make things happen.

The good news is prayer can be organized just like any other ministry! It does not have to be left up to chance. It need not be crisis-motivated. Rather, it can be done in simple obedience to the New Testament mandate. Here are some suggestions that can make your church more effective in prayer:

1. Begin praying for a spirit of prayer to fall on your church. Ask the Holy Spirit, the instigator of all prayer, to raise up intercessors.
2. Ask God to give your church a burden for the lost and a vision for reaching the city.
3. Be committed to developing a lasting, qualitative prayer ministry that is Christ-motivated and not crisis-motivated.
4. Do whatever it takes to bring your pastor and leadership on board. Their blessing and support is critical.
5. Set realistic, measurable goals. For example, set a goal of having 10% of your membership involved in a prayer ministry in 12 months.
6. Select a prayer coordinator and/or prayer committee to handle the details. Do not assign to the pastor either of these roles.
7. Have periodic pledge campaigns in which people can commit to pray, and then schedule them. Do not expect people to pray in the same ministry until Jesus comes. Establishing a term for prayer builds in fulfillment with a sense of accomplishment.
8. Have training sessions for the prayer ministry. This can be done through Sunday School classes, special seminars and workshops, retreats, and even worship services. Budget for this in the church's financial planning.

Resources:

Churches That Pray
C. Peter Wagner

Pray the Price Resource Kit
Acts 29
Terry Teykl

Power House
Glen Martin, Dian Ginter

9. Provide a variety of prayer opportunities to include all who want a place to pray and then offer feedback and appreciation to those who participate.

10. Realize the obstacles to prayer. Satan will do all he can to stop you, so expect fallout, resistance and negative reactions.

This last point is so important, because prayer can be one of the hardest activities to get started in a church. It is amazing what kinds of excuses you might hear. Let me share some that are typical:

1. "I once prayed for my Aunt Martha's arthritis to get better and it didn't. I just don't think prayer works."
2. "I'll start praying once I get my life straightened out."
3. "We never have done anything like this before. Why start now?"
4. "I just think we need to have a board meeting about it and decide what action to take."
5. "I have too much to worry about myself right now to be worrying about other people's problems."
6. "I'm too busy."

Do not get discouraged. Simply be persistent and keep praying until you see a breakthrough. As one pastor said, starting prayer ministries is a little bit like starting to take vitamins. You can not expect to see visible results right away, but you will definitely feel the difference in the long run.

Many churches are finding that it is only when they commit to elevate prayer to the same organizational and financial status as other key programs in the church that they begin to see the fruit of praying the price. One Lutheran church in Phoenix, Arizona got so serious about prayer that they developed a full-scale college of prayer offering over 100 courses. Members and non-members alike can work toward a B.A., M.A., or Ph.D. certificate in prayer. Imagine the difference that kind of training would make in the prayer life of your church!

It is not enough for the pastor to pray fervently, nor is it sufficient for a leadership team to pray ardently on behalf of the congregation. Until the church owns prayer as a world-class weapon in the battle against evil and cherishes prayer as a means of intimate and constant communication with God, the turn-around efforts of a body are severely limited, if not altogether doomed, to failure.
-George Barna

Mobilizing to Pray

What if...

...every law enforcement officer, every local government official, and every judge in your city had at least one intercessor praying for protection and Godly wisdom for them on a daily basis?

...every Christian in your city committed to pray weekly for salvation to come to each house on their street?

...all of the churches across your city could worship together in city-wide rallies, proclaiming loyalty to Jesus instead of denominational groups?

...the schools, principals, and gangs in your city could each be prayed for by name 24 hours a day?

Your city can be prayed for, if you are willing to take the initiative and pray the price! But, as Francis Frangipane says, it will take a city-wide church to win a city-wide war. We must raise up *the church* so that our message is clear—Jesus. Here are some keys to mobilizing Christians in your city to stand in the gap.

1. Begin by studying strategies of one of the many cities in which cooperative prayer is already a reality.
2. Ask God for a vision for your city. Learn about the history of the area because it often yields insights into particular walls that need to come down or corporate sin issues that need to be dealt with.
3. Develop a strategy that fits your city and its unique resources and characteristics. Do not simply emulate what another city did to bring results. Seldom does God operate with a formula.
4. Create a plan of action with specific goals and objectives, a time line, and a list of pastors or leaders who might help herald the call.
5. Share the plan with every church in your city, if possible. Identify the "convening church(es)," those which are anointed to bring others together, and bring these key players on board.
6. Find a city-wide coordinator who will oversee and organize the mechanics. Having a recognized leader not only helps facilitate good communication, it also gives the ministry direction and credibility.
7. Be determined to include as many churches as possible. Denominationalsim or racism have absolutely no place in a true city-wide prayer ministry.
8. Establish a covenant fund so that all the churches can help

Resources:

Loving Your City into the Kingdom
Ted Haggard, JackHayford

Healing America's Wounds
Taking Our Cities for God
John Dawson

support the effort as they are able.

9. Establish a public prayer place that can be open 24 hours a day. Equip the room with pertinent information about prayer needs of the city and how to pray. Create a special prayer map for the area. Encourage people from any church to sign up to pray there one hour a week.

10. Be creative.

The Prayer Coordinator

Since I have mentioned that both your church and your city need to have prayer coordinators, let me suggest some qualities to look for when filling this position, and some of the responsibilities that he/she might carry.

Qualifications:

1. strong personal prayer life
2. spiritual maturity
3. gifts to organize, encourage, lead and communicate
4. good reputation in their home congregation and confidence of church leaders and other pastors
5. enough time to attend key prayer events
6. not a pastor!

Responsibilities:

1. Identify key people and enlist their support.
2. Gather a wide array of resources on prayer.
3. Research the church's/city's current prayer ministries.
4. Help develop and oversee the implementation of the plan.
5. Involve others in leadership roles.
6. Develop an information network.
7. Work closely with pastors and leaders to receive prayer, vision and guidance.
8. Encourage prayer involvement beyond the local church.

Imagine this...

Last year in Tuscon, Arizona, 30 different churches teamed up for Operation Blessing to feed approximately 2,000 homeless and poor in their city. They plan to hold the event annually, building it to involve both secular and Christian agencies.

City conveners are not self appointed. They have:
tenure
respect
humility
wisdom
blessing
favor

1. On a scale of one to ten rate your personal prayer life. What is good about it. What might you incorporate from pages 26 and 27?

2. Who in your church, if anyone, is responsible for promoting prayer? Do you know who the "convening churches" are in your town?

3. What is the number one obstacle to prayer in your church? It might be interesting for you to research the part prayer played in your church's history.

4. In the last year what events have taken place in your city that focused on prayer? Who participated?

5. What would it take to bring many churches together for a city-wide prayer effort? What are the first 5 things you would do if you were assigned that task?

In Closing: Ask God to work in the hearts of the influential churches and pastors in town so that they might herald the cause of unity.

Jesus went through all the towns and villages, teaching in their synagogues, preaching the good news of the Kingdom, and healing every disease and sickness.   Matt. 9:35

Notes

Qualifications of a prayer coordinator:

1. Well respected in the community;
2. A person who carries and presents himself or herself honorably;
3. A person who possesses and practices personal integrity;
4. One who meets the biblical qualifications for eldership;
5. Someone who is willing to follow the lead of the churches and balance infusing them with fresh ideas;
6. A person with enough backbone to keep things moving in unity, but not arrogant or haughty;
7. One who would never appoint himself or herself;
8. Someone who has lived in the city at least 10 years with a good reputation among those who know him or her;
9. A man or woman who avoids church/pastoral/servant-ministry moods or quibbles. Someone the leaders listen to, but one who does not talk too much. A good listener, yet a quality speaker.
10. Someone who laughs easily.

Taken from *Loving Your City into the Kingdom*, by Ted Haggard and Jack Hayford

Nothing is discussed more and practiced less than prayer.   -Anonymous

Essential Unity

At a large Promise Keepers meeting, 42,000 pastors gathered in the Georgia Dome to hear Max Lucado, a well-known author and Church of Christ pastor. He used a very simple, but clever illustration to drive home a point. First, he asked the men to shout out, in unison, the church from which they came. Of course, the answer was a jumbled discord of denominational tags. Then he asked them, "Who saved you?" The one word reply shook the stadium, "Jesus!"

Jesus said in Matthew 12:25 that a divided house can not stand. In other words, as Christians, if we allow our theology or style of worship to keep us at odds with each other, we will have a difficult time impacting our cities for God. Perhaps that is why in John 17:23 Jesus prayed, "May they be brought to complete unity to let the world know that you sent me."

As you read through Jesus' prayer in the first 26 verses of John 17, you will see that Jesus prayed for seven things:

1. ...to be glorified in the churches (v. 1).
2. ...for the churches to be protected (v. 11).
3. ...for us to be sanctified and cleansed by the truth (v. 17).
4. **...for His people to be one** (v. 21-23).
5. ...that the churches would have power to save the lost (v. 20).
6. ...that the destiny of the church would be fulfilled with a heavenly vision (v. 24).
7. ...that His Father would be revealed to the churches (v. 26).

Some time ago, as I was meditating on that passage, God impressed upon me to stop praying these verses and begin answering them! As churches, I believe it is our responsibility to become the solution. For example, in El Paso, Texas seventy churches pooled their resources to purchase billboards naming 1997 "The Year of the Bible." They give free Bibles to anyone who calls the telephone number on the signs, and they are leading about fifty percent of the callers to Christ! In Cedar Rapids, Iowa several congregations meet together on the first Saturday of each month to worship in a different church according to that style. They call it "First Light." In Modesta, California the churches are so unified in purpose and in prayer that many of them have changed their signs to read, "The Church of Modesta." Their denominational labels are merely a subscript or have been taken off altogether. And in Colorado Springs, Colorado 140 churches have signed a "Declaration of Interdependence," stating their need for each other and their desire to work together.

Resource:
The Emerging American Church
Dan Scott

36

This move toward unity in the body of Christ is astounding. I sense that we are entering a time in which denominational labels are going to give way to the preeminance of the name of Jesus. Just imagine every Christian in your city, in every church, praying for the same things. Imagine pastors praying together, churches coming together for concerts of prayer and city-wide schools of prayer. It is happening all over the country. The spirit of parochialism is fast receding while the spirit of unity and cooperation is rising like leaven in city after city.

An important outgrowth of this move toward unity is the ever increasing number of pastors' prayer groups springing up. In city after city, pastors are laying down their competitive attitudes and reaching out across all kinds of denominational and racial boundaries to encourage, feed and lean on each other. They are gathering to pray for each other, fast for their cities, seek repentance for past sins or wrong attitudes, share in communion and wait on a corporate vision from God. As leaders, they are realizing that there is really only one church with many different expressions, and that they desperately need each other in order to advance God's Kingdom where they live.

"The Lord said, 'If as one people speaking the same language they have begun to do this [build a great tower], then nothing they plan to do will be impossible for them'" (Genesis 11:6). What "impossible" tasks could be accomplished in your city if all the Christians were "speaking the same language" instead of speaking criticism toward each other?

Covenant of Unity

The following is an excerpt from a Covenant of Unity signed by churches in Tampa Bay, Florida:

We believe Jesus Christ has one Church. The Church...in the Bay Area is comprised of many believers and congregations. Endeavoring to keep the unity of the Spirit in the bond of peace, we solemnly and joyfully enter into this covenant, pledging that by God's grace we shall:

◆ Advertise in a manner which is positive for the whole Bride of Christ, and not self-promoting at the expense of other churches or ministries.
◆ Respect and pursue relationships with those who are different doctrinally, denominationally, and racially....
◆ Be real and transparent with one another, resisting the temptation to impress each other with our site, abilities, or accomplishments.

Imagine this...

In Spokane, Washington on September 29, 1996, 116 churches met for a reconciliation service seeking God's forgiveness for the sins of their past.

When the tide rises, all the ships are raised equally.

Essential Unity

The USA men's basketball team has been dubbed the "Dream Team" because it is comprised of the best players from each team in the NBA. As opponents, none of these players can dominate completely. But as teammates, with all their skills working in symphony, they are unarguably the best in the world. No one else can even come close.

Sometimes I think as the body of Christ, we have been divided for so long that we no longer sense the division or realize what it is costing us. In many ways, we are paying a high price for our superior attitudes and denominational pride. We are so busy battling each other that we are losing ground in the war for our neighborhoods and towns. But when we combine our strengths, and begin to play in harmony with each other, the effectiveness of our ministries is multiplied way beyond what any of us could do on our own. For several reasons, unity among us is critical to our mission.

1. Our love for each other gives credibility to our message.

Think about this: Would you accept marital advice from a person who was in the middle of their sixth divorce? Would you accept tax advice from a friend who is in trouble with the IRS?

How can we expect non-believers to be drawn to Jesus if those who proclaim to be His followers do more backbiting than loving? How appealing is Christianity to a lost world when its messengers seem to be their own worst enemies?

Remember Jesus' prayer, "May they be brought to complete unity to let the world know that you sent me and have loved them...." He knew that the Father's love could only be demonstrated to the world if it was first practiced by those who already know Him. Those who are hurting without Jesus will be drawn to Him by our testimony of love for each other. Therefore, the more we can encourage and build up all who are in the family of God, the better our witness will be to those who are not yet in the fold.

2. We really only have one message: Jesus.

The disciples did everything in the name of Jesus, for the name of Jesus and through the name of Jesus. In fact, in the book of Acts alone, the name of Jesus is mentioned at least 33 times. As they traveled from town to town preaching, there was no confusion as to their message because they had no hidden agendas.

This may be a difficult concept for some to digest, but it is truth. If our time and energy is spent recruiting new members in order to build our own church or denominational name, then we are missing the mark. Bringing in new people to your church is a wonderful thing, especially if

Resource:
The House of the Lord
Francis Frangipane

they are new converts. But our hearts must be for calling people to Jesus Christ, regardless of which church they ultimately make their home.

3. We have strength in diversity.

Our differences are one of our greatest assets when it comes to reaching our cities with the Gospel. Ted Haggard says it this way in his book, *Primary Purpose*:

> Our primary purpose does not require every church to reach every person. It would be impossible. God would not allow it because it would violate His establishment of the body. Instead God requires us to reach a specific group effectively and helps us understand that a different flavor in the body of Christ is our co-worker to reach still another group. Through the strength we draw from our different flavors, we can communicate to the various people within our communities.

4. We have strength in numbers.

The only reason an individual police officer has any authority is that he has the support of the entire law enforcement department behind him. Likewise, our spiritual authority is grounded in the position we hold as members of the body of Christ. When we try to act on our own, our spiritual authority is dramatically weakened.

This is especially true in the area of spiritual warfare. Trying to do battle in the heavenly realms without the support of our brothers and sisters is a kamikaze mission. Sometimes we can even do more harm than good. We need to be united with the rest of the body before we confront sin and darkness.

5. God promises us power in agreement.

Jesus made it clear that we have power in agreement, saying, "Again, I tell you that if two of you on earth agree about anything you ask for, it will be done for you by my Father in heaven. For where two or three come together in my name, there am I with them."

Something about the act of agreement between believers clears the way for God's power to be released and for the Holy Spirit to work. It might be important for us to ask ourselves the question, "If power lies in agreement, what is the result of disagreement?"

Imagine this...

In one city, in response to one pastor's vision, several pastors prayed and fasted together for 21 days over two, five-gallon spray bottles filled with olive oil. Then, dressed in work clothes, they sprayed the ground around several of the most immoral establishments in their city, praying for God to intervene. Over the next year, over 50% of the places closed down.

The Blackaby Principle: Instead of creating your own agenda and then asking God to bless it, find out what God is blessing and get on board.

Essential Unity

The concept of "team" is a very important one to keep in mind as you work to develop unity among the churches in your city. Creating a city-wide church is a little like putting together an all-star team of players who wear different colored jerseys and work from a diffferent playbook. At first, working in sync may seem impossible.

But consider this: America's "Dream Team" was motivated by one thing—gold. It was their corporate vision, and they were willing to lay aside personal goals and accolades in order to reach it together. The thought of watching the American flag ascend in the stadium to the pulse of the *Star-Spangled Banner* ignited a comradery in them that superceded who they were as individuals.

Likewise, unity among the churches in your city will grow stronger as together, you rally around a corporate vision. Just as the Holy Spirit gives to each individual church a vision that charts their course and gives rise to specific goals and objectives, He also wants to reveal a vision to the city-wide church as it matures. I believe this is what Jesus meant when he told the disciples, "...open your eyes and look at the fields! They are ripe for harvest." He wanted them to catch the vision—*His* vision—for that city.

Of course, the ultimate vision has really already been given. Jesus told us to make disciples of all men. So when we talk about seeking a vision, what we are really saying is, "Set your sights on His vision for your city, and then ask Him to reveal the strategy that you can follow to accomplish it." God knows exactly what He wants to do in your local high schools, neighborhoods, workplaces and governments, and He already knows how He will bring it to pass. He simply desires your cooperation.

Eventually, the corporate vision can be shared by every church member in your city, but understand that it really must originate within the pastors and leaders. That is why the idea of pastors praying together is so critical to the development of unity. Another thing you must realize is that you can never fabricate a true vision, nor can you coerce the Holy Spirit into revealing one. However, the pastors in your city can do several things to posture themselves to be ready to receive it.

1. Build relationships. This is fundamental to the team concept.
2. Pray and fast together. In the Metroplex between Dallas and Fort Worth, 180 pastors fasted for forty days as they sought a corporate vision for their area.
3. Spend time together waiting quietly on the Lord. This can be done in special prayer retreats, prayer summits or weekly prayer meetings. Remember in Acts 1, Jesus told the disciples not to do

Resource:

Reunitus
Joe Aldrich

anything, but to wait in the Upper Room until they had received the Holy Spirit. For the Holy Spirit is the true Evangelist, and He is our helper in prayer (Rom. 8:26).

He is our instigator (Acts 1:2, 14).
He is our edifier (Jude 20, 1 Cor. 14:4).
He is our warner (Acts 20:23).
He is our revealer (John 14:26, 15:26).
He is our guide (Acts 13:4).
He is our source of joy (Luke 10:21).

4. Engage in corporate repentance. Past sins and hurts may need to be addressed before unity can take hold.
5. Submit to one another. This involves accepting the leadership roles that will inevitably arise out of time together.

In some cities, as I have already mentioned, the concept of a city-wide church is fairly developed. Colorado Springs, Colorado is leading the way. The churches there have decided to make it "the hardest city in America to go to hell from," and their story is told in Ted Haggard's book *Primary Purpose.*

Because the churches in Colorado Springs were committed to a shared vision, they became very creative in finding strategies to bring it to pass. One idea they have implemented is that of assigning various people groups, such as lawyers, factory workers, housewives, students, truckers, and so forth, to individual churches to be prayed for daily. Each church is then able to focus their energy on how they can reach their particular group. The exciting thing is that all the churches can rejoice over new converts, regardless of which congregation they choose to attend, because as the larger body of Christ, they have all had a part in praying the new believers into the Kingdom.

There are different kinds of gifts, but the same Spirit. There are different kinds of service, but the same Lord. There are different kinds of working, but the same God works all of them in all men.   I Cor. 12:4-6

● ●

1. What are the positive signs of unity in your area? Do you know of any pastors' groups that are praying together?

2. What ministry outreach in your city would be more effective if done as a corporate effort?

3. What is the number one obstacle to unity between the churches in your city? What absolutes of the faith could the churches use as common ground?

4. Are there racial or denominational walls in your city? Are there events in your city's history that caused that division?

5. Could the idea of unity in the body of Christ be frightening? Why?

In Closing: Pray through John 17.

From him the whole body, joined and held together by every supporting ligament, grows and builds itself up in love, as each part does its work.   Ephesians 4:16

March for Jesus Quick Facts

1. **Total number of marchers worldwide** - estimated 6 million
2. **Total number of nations marching** - over 100
3. **Total number of U. S. cities participating** - 700
4. **Total number of marchers in the U. S.** - 1 million
5. **States declaring May 17, 1997 as "March for Jesus Day":** Alabama, Florida, Louisiana, Nebraska, Nevada, New York, South Dakota, Tennessee, Texas
6. **Largest March in the world**- Sao Paulo, Brazil: 1.5 million
7. **Largest Marches in U. S.-**
   Nashville, TN - 40,000
   Oklahoma City, OK - 20,000
   Panama City, FL - 15,000
   Youngstown, OH - 13,000
   Pittsburgh, PA - 12,000
   Austin, TX - 10,000
8. **Future Marches:**
   May 30, 1998
   May 22, 1999
   June 10, 2000

Taken from *Church Without Walls*, 1997 March for Jesus Report

---

Prayer is the slender nerve that moves the muscle of omnipotence.   -Charles Spurgeon

---

Acts 29

In my early years as a pastor, one of my favorite places to go to be alone with God was a hunting cabin outside of town. One Saturday while I was there, God spoke a message so clearly to me that it has directed my entire ministry ever since. He told me to "build the church in prayer." Although I did not completely understand at the time what that meant, I determined that if I accomplished nothing else as a pastor, I would do everything I could to make Aldersgate UMC a praying church.

Over the next several years, our church held regular prayer vigils and our people were diligent about holding early morning prayer meetings wherever they could assemble. The more we prayed, the more we grew in number and the more we saw the Holy Spirit move.

Not long after we moved into a new building, we were holding a season of early morning prayer when a math professor in my church named Mark pulled me aside one Sunday morning. He shared with me that as he had been praying in the mornings, he had been reading through the book of Acts, one chapter each day, asking God to do the same things in our church and city. I liked the concept. I knew the value of praying scripture and of praying systematically, so I decided to try it myself.

I quickly became immersed in the life of the early church. I sat in the back of the Upper Room in Acts 1:14, and I watched the lame man jump to his feet in Acts 3. I walked with the disciples from city to city, listening to them pray. I went to the roof with Peter, and stood by him as he was accused and persecuted. I was literally swept away by their fervent prayer life as I saw the revelation of the Great Commission through their eyes. They did not hold prayer meetings; they were one. They had no money, no resources, no buildings and no music program. They had nothing except a vision for their city and an unbelievable prayer life. Yet they carried the Gospel from the Upper Room to every living room in Jerusalem and beyond.

The drama spelled out in those pages reached out and grabbed me and threw me down in a headlock. I was inspired by their zeal, and in nearly every chapter I found a powerful prayer for my own city simply by reading the testimonies of the disciples and saying, "Lord, do it again!" I realized that cities had not changed, sin had not changed, and God had not changed. All of the mass conversions and miracles that the early church saw in the book of Acts could still happen today.

So gripped was I by the way the Spirit worked in response to their prayers, that I continued to read through Acts over and over again, chapter by chapter. It became a regular part of my daily devotional time. And over the next several months and years, I read, studied and prayed with the disciples.

The more I read, the more I began to notice two things: (1) The book seemed to be unfinished, and (2) Ten prayer models emerged as the basics of the disciples' corporate prayer life and ministry.

Acts 29

If you read to the end of Acts 28, you will notice that it has no formal closing like the other letters in the New Testament. It does not say, "...to the only wise God be glory forever through Jesus Christ! Amen" (Rom. 16:27), or "Peace to the brothers..., and grace to all who love our Lord Jesus Christ with an undying love" (Eph. 6:23-24). Instead, the final verse in Acts reads, "Boldly and without hindrance he [Paul] preached the kingdom of God and taught about the Lord Jesus Christ."

I consulted several commentaries which suggested that the ending to Acts had been lost. But then I consulted God. He impressed upon my spirit that Acts has no ending because it is not yet finished! The Holy Spirit is still working in cities today just as He did in Jerusalem, Ephesus, Corinth, and others. The first 28 chapters are simply testimonies of what can happen when we apply the ten models of prayer to the Great Commission. God's desire is that every community in every city across the globe would be writing Acts 29 today.

Strategic Prayer Models

Throughout the 28 chapters of Acts, I identified ten prayer models that made up the disciples' corporate prayer life:

1. They had established places and times of prayer.
2. They prayed for leaders.
3. They saw prayer as a ministry.
4. They engaged in various types of corporate prayer.
5. They often prayed in homes.
6. They prayed as they walked.
7. They were open to praying at any time, any place.
8. They frequently fasted and prayed.
9. They prayed before they worshipped or preached.
10. They occasionally prayed authoritatively against evil.

As I studied them, I realized that these ten models are like blueprints that we need to build a house of prayer, and it is these ten models that are springing up all over the world today.

With that in mind, I pray these models will become the blueprints for your church's prayer life, and that they will serve as an Acts 29 challenge to engage you in strategic prayer for apostolic results in your city.

> *Imagine this...*
>
> *A woman from my church decided to practice Acts 29 praying so she picked out a tavern in town that was notorious for drunkenness and immorality, and began doing weekly drive-by praying. Several months later, she came to my office with a snapshot in her hand, grinning. It was a picture of the club, which had been bought out and renamed "Praise the Lord Beauty Salon."*

> *If the world hates you, keep in mind that it hated me first;*
> *If they persecuted me, they will persecute you also.*
> *-Jesus*

1. What were the qualities that made the early church effective in evangelism?

2. What would happen to the church at large if all of the buildings and pastors disappeared?

3. Compare the cities in the book of Acts to the cities of today.

4. Where in your city is Acts 29 being written?

5. What is the purpose of a blueprint?

In Closing: Welcome the Holy Spirit to come and help take the city for God.

Allow yourself and your church to take prayer as seriously as you take education, worship, outreach and fellowship.
    -C. Peter Wagner

God promises to bless anyone who blesses Israel.
Pray for the peace of Jerusalem.   Psalm 122:6

1. For Jerusalem to remain as Israel's undivided capital.
2. For God to remove the veil for them to see Jesus as the Messiah.
3. For peace between religious and secular Jews.
4. For deliverance from religious spirits.
5. For the peace between believers, especially Jewish and Arab believers.
6. For the Body of Messiah to become a praying, maturing body.
7. For Christian leaders.

From "A Call for 40 Days of Prayer and Fasting for Jerusalem" by Intercessors for America

The more praying there is in the world, the better the world will be; the mightier the forces against evil everywhere.   -E. M. Bounds

Making Room To Pray

Read Acts 1:1-14; 4:23-31; 16:13-34

Jesus said, "My house will be called a house of prayer" (Matt. 21:13). My eyes were opened to the true meaning of that verse when I visited Korea several years ago and witnessed a lifestyle of prayer that is literally foreign to us as Americans. I toured Prayer Mountain, where hundreds of Christians come to seek God in tiny "grottos." I attended several early morning prayer services with thousands of others who came daily at 4:00, 5:00 and 6:00 a.m. to engage in corporate prayer for one hour before going to work. And I visited churches where revival was the "norm" due to the incredible prayer force that was constantly being offered up somewhere in the building. At home, we were doing good just to get our people to pray for ten minutes on Sunday morning! I was convicted and challenged by the realization that we were really missing the boat in the area of prayer.

God used that experience to instill in me a passion for prayer rooms, and I immediately put one in our new church building. I knew that if ongoing, fervent prayer was going to be developed, it needed a place to happen. God had given us a great task, but like the disciples, He expected us to seek Him with all our hearts and souls and strength before we endeavored to do it. He did not intend for us to accomplish it in any way except through prayer.

What is a Prayer Room?

Every prayer room I have ever seen is different—some are big, and some are small; some are elaborate, and some are simple. They vary in appearance just as much as church buildings do. However, most prayer rooms do have several things in common:

They are in a place that offers privacy. I have helped put prayer rooms into former classrooms, unused offices, junk rooms, empty storage closets, portable buildings, chapels—just about any space that can be closed off from outside distractions.

They are comfortable. Prayer rooms should be inviting places to sit, kneel, or even lay prostrate before the Lord and enjoy His presence. Comfortable chairs, carpet, tables, plants, adequate lighting, sufficient ventilation, pillows, and wall hangings will help create a pleasant atmosphere.

They are inspirational and informative. I encourage churches to organize their prayer rooms into stations, displaying helpful information to guide people as they pray. For example, our prayer room contained twelve stations that included time for praise, thanksgiving, waiting and petitioning. We provided information about our city such as the

Resource:
Making Room to Pray
Terry Teykl

names of schools, city officials, principals, high crime areas, gangs, hospitals and media sources. We also made available special prayer requests from our congregation, the pastoral staff, and the community.

If possible, they are safely accessible 24 hours a day. This means they have an outside entrance, are equipped with a combination lock and a telephone, and are well-lighted.

They are used on an individual, sign-up basis. We had prayer pledges during which our people could sign up to pray in the prayer room one hour each week for a term of three months. Privacy needs to be respected, though some may choose to come with a prayer partner or spouse. Some parents were blessed by bringing their children.

Imagine this...

First Congregational Church in Hopkinton, Massachusetts takes up business cards during the worship services and puts them in their prayer room in a notebook called "Abraham's Blessings." Intercessors pray over each card for prosperity so that the work of the Kingdom might be blessed.

Advantages of Prayer Places

1. They make it possible to schedule prayer.
2. They promote agreement in prayer by providing a place where information can be gathered and prayed over.
3. They offer a place to record the deeds of God, lest we neglect to thank Him and praise Him for all He does.
4. They make a statement to the community about the importance of prayer.
5. They provide a place where prayer can be practiced and matured.
6. They are inclusive—anyone can pray in a prayer room.
7. They act as "hearing aids" for church leadership.
8. They provide a place where serious concerns can be soaked in prayer.
9. They minister the presence of God to those who come.
10. They provide a "control center" for strategic prayer evangelism, warfare and other prayer ministries.

Tallowood Baptist Church spends $20,000 a year on printing materials for their prayer room.

The Bible says, "And will not God vindicate his elect who cry out to him day and night?" Hundreds of churches across the country are seeing dramatic results from setting aside places for intentional, ongoing, consistent prayer.

For Group Discussion

1. Is there a prayer room in your church? Are there any prayer places in your city?

2. If not, where could one be established? If so, are they being used to their fullest potential?

3. Describe a time when you felt in close communion with God.

4. How might having a prayer room in your church encourage other prayer ministries?

5. How do prayer rooms promote agreement in prayer?

In Closing: If your church does not have a prayer room, pray as a group that God would bring this to pass.

Prayer is not simply getting things from God, that is a most initial form of prayer; prayer is getting into perfect communion with God.   -Oswald Chambers

Prayer Application
Week #1 - Thy Kingdom Come

DAY ONE
Read and pray Matthew 6:9-13

As you go, preach this message: The Kingdom of heaven is near. Heal the sick, raise the dead, cleanse those who have leprosy, drive out demons. Freely you have received, freely give.   Matthew 10:7-8

DAY TWO
Read John 17

Beseech Jesus for the following churches to be one:

Repent in behalf of your city for things in the past causing divisions:

DAY THREE
Read Matthew 21:21

Pray John 17
Ask God for Jesus to be glorified in specific areas of your city government:

Ask God to fill these pastors with the Holy Spirit:

DAY FOUR
Read Matthew 21:1-13

Entreat God to release a spirit of prayer in your church and city.

Seek Him to raise up...
            prayer...intercessors..prayer groups...places of prayer

DAY FIVE
Read Acts 1:1-14, 16:13, 16:25

Talk to the Lord about your own personal place of prayer in your home.

DAY SIX
Read II Chronicles 6:12-42

Intercede at a known place of prayer such as a sanctuary, scenic overlook or high place in your area. Claim your city for God.

Anoint an entrance to your city with oil symbolizing the presence of the Holy Spirit.

DAY SEVEN
Read Psalm 107:1-15

Praise Him for what He has begun in your city.

Sing unto the Lord a song of thanksgiving.

Personal Reflections and Answers to Prayer:

Satan's Attacks on Prayer Rooms and God's Defense:

1. ***Destruction*** - Pray God's protection over the prayer room. Take authority over Satan in the strong name of Jesus, binding him with the blood of our Lord.
2. ***Indifference*** - Ask God to raise up enough intercessors and reserves to fill each hour.
3. ***Enshrinement*** - Pray that God will never let us become more impressed with the ministry than with Him. Ask God to help you look only to Him, giving Him the glory.
4. ***Carnal Intercessors*** - Pray that God will have full control over every intercessor's life.
5. ***Indiscretion*** - Pray that God will cause us to set a guard on our mouths. Nothing will destroy the intercessory prayer ministry as quickly as our gossiping about people's problems and needs. Do not share these needs with anyone once you leave the prayer room unless you have permission to do so. This matter is crucial. The effects are disastrous (Proverbs 16:28, 17:9, 18:8, 26:20, 22).

Taken from *Prayer Room Policies* by Terry Teykl

Suddenly a sound like the blowing of a violent wind came from heaven and filled the whole house where they were sitting.   Acts 2:2

Preyed On or Prayed For
Model #2

Read Acts 2

One of the ironies of life is that we sometimes tend to overlook that which should be most obvious. We remember Christmas gifts for everyone in the office but forget our wife's birthday. Or we get home from the grocery store and realize that we got everything except the most important item on the list.

It seems obvious to me that as the spiritual leaders of God's people, pastors should be high on our prayer list. Yet over the years, I have concluded that in many churches, the pastor is the least prayed for person in the congregation! In fact, it is no great wonder that the casualty rate is so high among clergy when the very people they serve often do more to attack them than to bless them.

Pastor neglect is a serious problem because not only does it work against a church's effectiveness, it also dishonors God. The principle is this: How can we honor God whom we can not see, when we can not even honor His appointed representative whom we can see? Exodus 17 tells a typical story of the relationship between a pastor and his people. As the Israelites set up camp at Rephidim, they encountered a shortage of drinking water and immediately they blamed Pastor Moses. How unfortunate it is that when something goes wrong in the church, our automatic reaction is to throw darts at the person behind the pulpit. How devastating it is to pastors and their families when they become so wounded by their own flock that they lose their zeal for ministry altogether.

Satan knows that if he can strike a shepherd, the sheep will scatter, and he loves nothing more than to see an effective spiritual leader fall. As a result, pastors need to be prayed for—not just in times of crisis or church difficulties—but consistently, intentionally and faithfully in every area of their lives. They need a hedge of protection both from "friendly fire" and from the darts that the enemy aims at their personal and family lives, their time with God, and their professional reputations. Think about this—it is almost impossible to criticize and pray for someone at the same time. Prayer releases in us the mercy and compassion of God. Therefore, by choosing to pray for your pastor, you are not only choosing to speak blessings, claiming all that God has for him or her, but you are also building a shield against all kinds of devices meant to halt or harm them. This pleases God!

In addition to being protected, pastors can also be built up and blessed by the prayers of their people. The apostle Paul, whose sermons inspired thousands to come to Christ, was a prayed-for preacher. He was prayed for consistently by those who knew of his ministry and he was prayed for especially as he spoke. You may have a pastor who is eloquent, educated and inspired. But imagine how much more powerful his or her

Resources:

Preyed On or Prayed For
Terry Teykl

Prayer Shield
C. Peter Wagner

Partners in Prayer
John Maxwell

preaching might be if coupled with a mighty prayer force behind the scenes. Just picture in your mind, as your pastor preaches on Sunday mornings, a group of intercessors in a back office praying for eyes to be opened, hearts to be receptive and lives to be changed. With prayer support like that, what happens in the service will be based on the work of the Holy Spirit, not on the pastor's performance that day. For most pastors, that spells relief!

Prayer Hedge Basics

1. Share your intentions with your pastor. Approach the idea with sensitivity, patience and gentle persistence.
2. Work with existing prayer ministries. Incorporate prayer for the pastor into Sunday school classes, small groups and other strong programs.
3. Recruit and train the intercessors. Research several good resources on pastoral prayer and equip intercessors to do the job right.
4. Find ways to pray for other pastors in your city as well. You will reap what you sow.

Caution!

Praying for your pastor is so critical that you can not afford to wait for approval from three committees, nor can you assume that if your pastor really needed prayer, he or she would have asked. Start praying today! Your pastor may not understand the importance of what you are doing at first, and may even be suspicious, but be sure to share your thoughts with him or her in a supportive, non-threatening way.

Work patiently and slowly to promote the idea of a prayer hedge and recruit mature, trustworthy intercessors. Be sensitive to the fact that your shepherd may be hesitant to reveal personal requests or needs until a trust relationship is built. For many pastors, receiving prayer can be difficult for several reasons: they may be dealing with spiritual pride, they may feel they do not deserve prayer, or they may simply be afraid to let anyone know they do not always have all their ducks in a row! And can we blame them? Pastors today live their lives teetering on platforms of high expectations, with virtually no safety net—all the more reason to hedge them in. Be prayerfully persistent, trusting God to open the way.

The Amalekites came and attacked the Israelites at Rephidim. Moses said to Joshua, "Choose some of our men and go out to fight the Amalekites. Tomorrow I will stand on top of the hill with the staff of God in my hands."
So Joshua fought the Amalekites as Moses had ordered, and Moses, Aaron and Hur went to the top of the hill. As long as Moses held up his hands, the Israelites were winning, but whenever he lowered his hands, the Amalekites were winning. When Moses' hands grew tired, they took a stone and put it under him and he sat on it. Aaron and Hur held his hands up...so that his hands remained steady till sunset. So Joshua overcame the Amalekite army with the sword.
Exodus 17:8-13

1. In the history of your church, has there been any pastor abuse or criticism?

2. Does any group or individual in your church make prayer for the pastor a priority?

3. Does your pastor share his or her prayer needs with anyone? Why or why not?

4. Where could prayer for the pastor begin in your church?

5. What are some things that could be done to begin prayer for the pastors of your city?

In Closing: Pray for your shepherd and pastoral staff.

There is nothing that makes us love a man so much as praying for him.   -William Law

Prayer Application
Week #2 - Your Pastor: Strong in the Lord and the Strength of His Might

DAY ONE
Read Acts 2

Invite the Holy Spirit to help you pray for your pastor.
Claim these promises for his or her protection:
> Isaiah 54:14-17
> Psalm 34:7
> Psalm 91
> Luke 10:19
> II Corinthians 10:3-4

DAY TWO
Read Isaiah 40:27-31, Romans 5:5

Seek God for your pastor's renewal and fresh infilling of the Holy Spirit.

Pray this prayer over your pastor:

> "Lord, make _____ strong and filled with courage for every task (Josh. 1).
> Let my pastor lead us to inherit our city for You. Thank you for being with him or her.
> Amen.

DAY THREE
Read Psalm 91:9-12, Psalm 37:5

Cancel in Jesus' name every assignment against your pastor's spouse, children, health, finances, etc.

Take authority over every obstacle to a rich and full ministry for Christ in your city (Matthew 10:1).

Request the Lord to give him or her a vision for your city (John 4:35).

DAY FOUR
Read Psalm 100

Thank God for your shepherd and the other shepherds of your city. Make a list of your pastor's strengths.

Write a prayer of encouragement to at least three pastors.

DAY FIVE
Read Acts 2:14-41

Pray for your pastor to preach like Peter with divine recall of scripture, timely messages, the anointing of the Holy Spirit, with boldness...

Ask God to grant him or her apostolic results.

Repent of any sins that your pastor preaches against (Acts 2:37).

DAY SIX
Read Acts 2:42-47

Supplicate the Lord to give right relationships to your pastor with other pastors.

Appeal to God for "pulpit swapping" in the city.

Ask God for a strong devotion to apostolic teaching, fellowship, breaking of the bread, and prayer among the brethren.

DAY SEVEN
Read Acts 4:23-31

Bless your pastor to be courageous and open to the new things of God.

Pray for him or her to stand in the middle of what the Spirit is doing in the land.

If possible, visit a worship service at a different church and pray for that pastor as he or she preaches.

Personal Reflections and Answers to Prayer:

Expectations on Today's Pastors

1. Live an exemplary life;
2. Be available at all times to all people for all purposes;
3. Lead the church to grow numerically;
4. Balance wisdom with leadership and love;
5. Teach people the deeper truths of the faith in ways that are readily applicable in all life situations;
6. Be a committed family man who demonstrates what it means to be the spiritual head of the family, a lover of one woman and a positive role model for children;
7. Keep pace with the latest trends and developments in church life;
8. Build significant relationships with members of the congregation;
9. Represent the church in the community;
10. Grow spiritually;
11. Run the church in a crisp, professional, business-like manner without taking on a cold, calculating air.

Taken from *Today's Pastors*
by George Barna.

Pray also for me, that whenever I open my mouth, words may be given me so that I will fearlessly make known the mystery of the gospel.... Ephesians 6:19

Prayer as a Ministry

Read Acts 3

The day that Jesus, in righteous indignation, drove the money changers and tax collectors from the temple, He was angry with what was taking place there. But I believe He was just as displeased, if not more, with what was *not* taking place there. I can just imagine Jesus approaching the temple, stepping over the lame and the lepers, pushing His way through the blind and the afflicted, all of whom had come hoping for a touch and a prayer, but had received nothing. As He turned over the tables and drove out those who were buying and selling, He said to them, "My house will be called a house of prayer...." And as soon as Jesus had cleared the temple, Matthew says, "The blind and the lame came to him..., and he healed them" (Matt. 21:14). Jesus wanted the people to be prayed for.

Early one Sunday morning before church, a lady walked into my office looking very troubled. She closed the door, sat down on the couch, and pulled a small handgun out of her purse. She had my full attention. She told me that she was extremely depressed, and that her situation was so bad she could find no reason to go on living. She said that she really did not want to die, but she needed someone to give her hope. I was her last resort.

I may not always have perfect discernment, but I instinctively knew that she was not interested in joining our women's group, baking pies for a potluck supper, or even hearing my sermon for that day. She did not care about our theological position on baptism, or whether we sang hymns or choruses. What she needed was an encounter with her heavenly Father. She needed to feel the powerful love of Jesus from the top of her head to the bottom of her feet.

Every Sunday, our churches are filled with people who are run over by life. They wear a smile on their face to hide the hurt of marital problems, abusive relationships, children who have turned away, financial failures and terminal illnesses. Week after week, they come to church desperately needing a touch from God, and often leave in the same condition in which they arrived. How tragic it is when broken humanity passes through our doors only to receive a bulletin and a nice, three-point sermon!

Action at the Altar

When we talk about prayer as a ministry, we are affirming John Wesley's belief in prayer as a "means of grace." If we are willing to be available to God simply by praying with someone who is hurting, He will use us as conduits of His mercy and love. Through us, He can minister healing, compassion, encouragement, hope, wisdom, courage or salvation. We do not have to produce anything ourselves; we just have to be

Resources:

That Ye May Know
Jerry Simmons

Intercessory Prayer
Dutch Sheets

"user friendly." God supplies the power.

This type of one-on-one prayer must not be confined to the church, but that is definitely where it should begin. It is time that we re-open our altars as places of intercession and personal ministry, and that we schedule plenty of time in our services for it to happen. If that means we have less time for announcements, or that we have to stay past 12:00 noon, or that the pastor has to give up 10 minutes of sermon time, so be it! Prayer should be the most important thing we do on Sunday mornings. For the lady with the handgun in her purse, and the hundreds of others like her, it is our means of connecting them to the Living God.

Many churches, in addition to praying at the altar, are finding creative ways to move prayer out into their communities in meaningful ways. Consider the following testimonies:

1. Community of Joy Church in Phoenix, AZ has developed a full-scale college of prayer, offering over 100 courses to bachelor, master and doctor of philosophy certificate candidates.
2. One Baptist church in Houston, TX has a 24-hour prayer hotline in their prayer room.
3. Voice of Pentecost Church in San Francisco, CA prays for every single home in the city once a year.
4. A Church of Christ in Pittsburgh, PA mobilizes prayer for hospital patients who do not list a church home.
5. Hillcrest Church in Dallas, TX has organized home prayer cells in nearly every zip code in that city.

Praying for the Sick

In Acts 3, Peter and John demonstrated prayer as a ministry of physical healing when they prayed for the lame beggar at the city gate called Beautiful. Not only did the beggar receive a special touch from God that day, but hundreds of people who lived in the city and heard the beggar's testimony believed in Jesus because of the miracle they witnessed!

Jesus was the healer. He demonstrated and taught the ministry of laying on of hands (Mark 1:31, 41, 6:13), and He commissioned His disciples to follow His example. Praying for the sick is a powerful testimony of faith, and we need not worry about the outcome. Remember, we are not the power supply, only the extension cord. If we simply minister in love, inviting the Holy Spirit to work, God will move in His sovereignty and glorify the Son.

Imagine this...

Over 650 police officers in the Houston Police Department receive prayer every day from their own personal intercessors. The program, called Shield A Badge, was started through the prayer ministries of Second Baptist Church in order to offer encouragement and prayer protection to the law enforcement personel whose lives are on the line every day.

The gift of intercession is the special ability that God gives to certain members of the Body of Christ to pray for extended periods of time on a regular basis and see frequent and specific answers to their prayers to a degree much greater than that which is expected of the average Christian.

-C. Peter Wagner

For Group Discussion

1. Have you ever been prayed for in a significant manner. When? Who prayed for you?

2. Why are people afraid of praying out loud?

3. Is there any time during your church service designated for people to receive the ministry of prayer?

4. Would your church be open to a prayer time at the altar?

5. Why do people tend to think the pastor is the only one who can pray for them? What can be done to establish a prayer ministry team in your church?

In Closing: Pray for one another's personal needs.

We are the womb of God upon the earth....We do not generate life, but we release, through prayer, Him who does.   -Dutch Sheets

Prayer Application
Week #3 - In Jesus' Name

DAY ONE
Ponder Acts 3

Worship God for giving us access to Him in Jesus' name (John 16:23).

Bow in praise that He has given us authority over evil in Jesus' name (Matthew 10:1).

Know that in the name of Jesus, we are forgiven and saved (Acts 4:12).

DAY TWO
Read James 5:13-16

Name the terminally ill and request healing for them in Jesus' name:

Intercede for physicians, technicians, hospitals, administrators, Christian counselors, etc. of the medical community in your city:

DAY THREE
Read John 14:12-14

Repent of not seeing or hearing the plight of the poor.

Imagine and pray for joint efforts between churches to feed and care for the needy.

Ask God to heal and minister to the needs of the HIV victims and their families.

DAY FOUR
Meditate on Isaiah 25:9

Declare the Lord to be the sole hope for your city.

Focus in prayer on the felt needs of the homeless for immediate relief, shelter, food, clothing, protection from danger, employment, and restored family life.

DAY FIVE
Review Matthew 21:1-14

Kneel at your church altar and ask God to meet felt needs there. List and pray for three people you know who have basic needs in their life.

Listen for the Spirit's leading in regard to opening up the altar during worship so that hurting people might receive prayer.

Bless the Lord for breaking the curse of poverty (Luke 4:18, Galatians 3:13-14).

DAY SIX
Read Matthew 25:31-46

Visit a jail to pray for the inmates and jailers, or...

Sit in the lobby of a nursing home and ask God to show you someone who needs to be loved on in the name of the Lord, or...

Find a hospital ICU waiting room or emergency room and simply pray for the people there to be comforted.

DAY SEVEN
Recite Psalm 23

Wait on the Lord in silence, reflecting on God's goodness.

Therefore God exalted him to the highest place and gave him the name that is above every name... Philippians 2:9

Personal Reflections and Answers to Prayer:

Sample Guidelines for Altar Workers

1. Come to the altar at the leading of the pastor.
2. Men pray with men, women pray with women.
3. Listen for a direction to pray. Do not be shocked by what you hear.
4. Ask for permission to pray.
5. Pray scriptures over the person.
6. Refer serious problems to the pastoral staff.
7. Take distressed people into a private place for prayer.
8. Have tissue boxes available.
9. Encourage team praying when possible. While one is speaking, the other prays.
10. Make pertinent materials available for those who receive prayer.

The apostles performed many miraculous signs and wonders among the people....[and] more and more men and women believed in the Lord....Acts 5:12,14

Corporate Prayer
Read Acts 4

Model **#4**

When I lived in College Station, Texas, home of Texas A&M University, one of my favorite places to jog was Kyle Field where the Aggies play football. Probably just as well known as the football team is their military style marching band that is the pride of A&M.

I watched them practice many times, and was always amazed at their precision and exactness. After they finished a drill you could see a grid of circles in the astroturf where their feet had all landed, because their steps were so carefully measured that they literally marched in each others' footprints.

One time as I was visiting with one of the drill leaders who went to my church, I commented on how impressed I was with their accuracy, and he said, "Yes, that is why when we march over a bridge, we instruct the cadets to intentionally break cadence." He explained that in physics, there is a principle known as "natural frequency" which basically says that a force on a structure that is repeated in exactly the same spot over and over, even if it is a small force, will eventually cause damage to the structure. In other words, the Aggie band could theoretically crumble a bridge just by marching on it, as long as they are in step with each other!

Corporate prayer is a spiritual application of the principle of natural frequency, and it calls into action the promise Jesus made in Matthew 18:19, "Again, I tell you that if two of you on earth agree about anything you ask for, it will be done for you by my Father in heaven." In corporate prayer, we pray in step with one another, and in agreement with God's Word for a specific outcome. It really does not even matter whether we are all seated in the same room or scattered about the city.

One of the best examples of corporate prayer in recent years has been the force of intercession aimed at the 10/40 Window. Thousands of people all over the world received information about what to pray, how to pray, and when to pray for the salvation of those living in that area. Although they were never actually all in one place, every person who prayed for the 10/40 Window was engaged in corporate prayer because as a whole, they were in agreement, and they were in step.

Corporate prayer has many expressions that have characterized the current prayer surge including Moms in Touch groups, Marches for Jesus, early morning prayer, the Watchman Prayer Ministry, prayer at the flagpole, and the three flagships of corporate prayer: prayer vigils, concerts of prayer, and solemn assemblies.

Prayer Vigils

A prayer vigil is a focused time of intense intercession for a spe-

Resource:

Concerts of Prayer
David Bryant

66

cific need or concern. They are often held in response to crises such as life-threatening illnesses, major decisions, tragedies in the community or serious circumstances in the church body. They apply the principle that if believers will earnestly pray through a situation with faith and persistence, they will see a breakthrough. Prayer vigils can range anywhere from one hour to several days in length, and usually involve people coming in uninterrupted shifts and praying according to a schedule of some kind (Acts 12:5).

Concerts of Prayer

Concerts of Prayer actually date back to the 1700's when a preacher organized his congregation into prayer cells which met weekly. Once a month the prayer cells would come together for corporate prayer, and then once a quarter, all the churches in the city would come together. They are typified by concerted prayer for global issues such as world evangelization and spiritual awakening. These prayer events usually last for one to several hours, and involve time for praise, instruction, thanksgiving, seeking, testimonies and of course, prayer.

Solemn Assemblies

A Solemn Assembly is a called time of corporate repentance and prayer based on the Old Testament model seen primarily in II Chronicles. In essence, it is an act of humility and brokenness by a people of God, identifying with the sins of a city or nation, seeking God's mercy and forgiveness to avoid judgment, and being restored to Him. They are often characterized by urgency and grief over sin which has offended God, scriptural readings, worship, and covenant. The movement exploded when, in 1994 the Southern Baptists had a three-hour Solemn Assembly on Wednesday night of their annual convention. In an unprecedented show of repentance and brokenness, the leaders of that denomination took a turn toward radical dependence on God (II Chron. 7:14).

Prayer is the most tangible trace of eternity in the human heart.
-Ed Silvoso

For *Group* *Discussion*

1. Describe the most meaningful prayer meeting you have ever attended. Describe the worst experience you have had at a prayer meeting.

2. Why is it important to have corporate prayer?

3. Does corporate prayer happen in your city? How often? Who leads it? Who participates?

4. How could you or your group initiate a concert of prayer in your city?

5. Take a moment right now and pray for corporate prayer to become a vital part of your church and your city.

In Closing: Practice corporate prayer in your group.

Answered prayer [is] the first test of a prayer meeting's effectiveness.   -Jack Hayford

Prayer Application
Week #4 - Praying Together

DAY ONE
Read Acts 4:23-31, Acts 12:5

Ask two or three friends to pray with you before your church service.

DAY TWO
Read and meditate on Matthew 18:19-20

Visit a corporate prayer meeting in your church.

DAY THREE
Read John 17:23

Attend a corporate prayer meeting in a church other than your own.

If you are a pastor, visit a pastors' prayer group in your town.

DAY FOUR
Read Acts 12

Join with a group of friends and call for prayer for persecuted Christians in the world. Research and prepare for this.

DAY FIVE

Read Psalm 103 with your spouse, your family, or a close friend.

List and offer up thanks for the following blessings in your city:

Thank God for these corporate expressions of prayer in your city:

DAY SIX

Read Galatians 6:7

Sow a book on corporate prayer to your pastor or church leader. For example, you could give them a copy of David Bryant's *Concerts of Prayer*.

DAY SEVEN

Read David's prayer in I Chronicles 29:10-19

Believe God to raise up expressions of corporate prayer in the following places:

O Lord, listen! O Lord forgive! O Lord, hear and act! For your sake, O my God, do not delay, because your city and your people bear your Name.   Daniel 9:19

Personal Reflections and Answers to Prayer:

Sample Guidelines for Corporate Prayer

1. Remember our goal - to submit ourselves and be sensitive to pray under the Holy Spirit's guidance.
2. Each individual's prayer should last 1 to 2 minutes.
3. Unless you have a very strong voice, come to the microphone to pray so we can all hear and "agree."
4. Pray the promises of scripture, but avoid reading long portions.
5. Focus on asking, not explaining. God already knows.
6. Avoid "preachy" praying.
7. Do not pray too big. Prayers for China or India are not suitable for corporate prayer because most people do not have faith for that, and can't be in agreement.
8. Silence is not a bad thing.
9. Come with faith.
10. When someone else is at the microphone, feel free to kneel or walk around, but do not disturb those around you.
11. Be listening, affirming, and agreeing with the intercession of the one at the microphone.
12. Keep in mind that this is not individual prayer.

Adapted from the Encourager Church in Houston, Texas

Humble yourselves before the Lord, and he will lift you up.   James 4:10

Houses of Prayer Everywhere

Read Acts 5

Model # 5

I was recently at a friend's house when a salesman came to his door. Listening in an adjacent room as the young man explained his mission, I knew right away my friend was in trouble. He would have saved himself and the young salesman a lot of time had he just given in right then. But my friend was not really interested in a magazine, so he resisted. But about fifteen minutes later, worn down and defeated, I heard the door close and my friend walked into the room holding a receipt for a twelve month subscription to a gardening periodical.

We have all done it—bought a magazine we will never read, a "magic" mop that we know will not work, a jar of candy we do not even like—simply because it was the only way to end the conversation! The sales method is called "hard-sell," and the strategy is, "Never take 'No' for an answer."

Unfortunately, I sometimes sense the same type of strategy behind evangelistic efforts. "You really are a terrible sinner and you need to get your life straight so that you can be a Christian like me. So open wide, here come the four spiritual laws." The problem is, people who respond to the Gospel presented in this manner probably do so for much the same reason that my friend bought the gardening magazine—to get rid of the salesman.

But perhaps "hard-sell" evangelism is not your problem because the very thought of talking to someone about Jesus makes your knees weak and your palms sweaty. Many Christians never experience the joy of leading another person to Christ because the whole idea seems awkward and embarrassing, and the fear of rejection is too overwhelming.

In the midst of this evangelism dilemma, a prayer evangelism ministry has emerged and is sweeping the country that is not only biblical, but gives temperance to the bold and boldness to the coward. It is called *Houses of Prayer Everywhere*, or *H.O.P.E.*, and it is a strategic way for Christians to make a tremendous difference in their neighborhoods and workplaces.

A House of Prayer is a cluster of two or more believers banded together to pray for and convey God's blessing upon those they work with and live around. The group may be composed of members of a household or several believers who meet together to pray. They are springing up everywhere—homes, apartment buildings, dorms, offices, schools, churches, factories—coupling the power of prayer with the warmth of face-to-face, personal interactions. They are effective because rather than one-shot, hard-sell tactics, they foster ongoing relationships and rely on earned trust.

The Houses of Prayer strategy progresses through five phases.

Resource:

Houses of Prayer Everywhere
Training Material
Alvin Vander Griend

72

In phase one, the members lay a foundation of prayer by interceding on behalf of neighbors. In phase two, indirect contact is made through door hangers, greeting cards and Prayer-a-Grams. In phase three, intercessors contact the neighbors directly to ask for prayer requests. And in phases four and five, the House of Prayer members share the Gospel with neighbors and invite them to church.

From the Upper Room to Every Living Room

The Book of Acts indicates that Houses of Prayer are not a new idea. Consider the following verses:

Acts 2:46b "They broke bread **in their homes** and ate together with glad and sincere hearts...."

Acts 5:42 "Day after day, in the temple courts and **from house to house**, they never stopped teaching and proclaiming the good news...."

Acts 9:11 "The Lord told him, '**Go to the house** of Judas on Straight Street and ask for a man from Tarsus named Saul....'"

Acts 10:22b, 23 "'A holy angel told him (Cornelius) to have you **come to his house** so that he could hear what you have to say.' Then Peter invited the men **into the house** to be his guests."

Acts 12:12 "...he **went to the house** of Mary the mother of John, also called Mark, where many people had gathered and were praying."

Acts 20:20 "You know that I have...taught you publicly and **from house to house**."

When Christians begin to pray for the felt needs of the lost, God surprises them with almost immediate answers to prayer. In fact, prayer for the needs of that one-hundredth sheep is the spiritual equivalent of dialing 911.
-Ed Silvoso

The apostles taught in homes and they prayed in homes. Ministering to the people in a household was significant in that culture partly because church buildings did not yet exist, and partly because the term "household" referred to the large extended families that typically lived together under one roof. When one person in a household received a touch from God, it was not unusual for the entire family, sometimes thirty or forty people, to accept the message of the Gospel, as in the case of the Roman jailer in Acts 16:29-34.

Houses of Prayer work! They enabled a rag-tag group of preachers to spread the message of a carpenter from Galilee throughout all of Jerusalem and into Asia Minor. Can you imagine the same thing happening on your street?

For Group Discussion

1. Describe some felt needs that you are aware of in your neighborhood.

2. Are you aware of any Houses of Prayer that meet in your area?

3. How many active church-goers live in your neighborhood? Do you know your immediate neighbors well enough to pray for them?

4. Why do the steps initiated in the House of Prayer strategy classify as "heart-sell" instead of "hard-sell"?

5. Would you attend a House of Prayer in your neighborhood? Would you host a House of Prayer in your neighborhood? Write the names of three people that you think would meet with you.

In Closing: Pray for your neighbors by name and need.

In Cedar Rapids, Iowa a lady began praying for her neighbors and within several months, her entire housing development was saved.

Prayer Application
Week #5 - Living in a Prayed For City

Read John 15:1-8

List the ways God has blessed your life and family.

Give thanks in all circumstances.... I Thessalonians 5:18

Recite John 15:7

Select three families on your street and pray for God to make Himself real to them in a unique way today:

Pray for their specific needs if known.

Read Matthew 28:16-20

Drive up and down your street praying for the homes to be filled with the presence of Christ.

Speak forgiveness and blessing on each home around you.

Read Genesis 12:1-3

Bless the three families you listed by naming them before God.

Ask God for an open door to pray for their felt needs.

DAY FIVE
Read II Chronicles 7:11-16

Intercede for forgiveness of any sins being committed in your neighborhood or community.

Listen quietly as you try to see your neighborhood as He sees it.

DAY SIX
Read Ephesians 6:10-20

Put the armor of God on the children that live close to you:

Invite a neighbor you do not know over for coffee or dinner.

DAY SEVEN
Read Psalm 145

Write a letter to the three families on your list and let them know you have been praying for them. In the letter, ask if they have any needs you could pray specifically for.

Personal Reflections and Answers to Prayer:

"Zacchaeus, come down immediately. I must stay at your house.... Today salvation has come to this house." Luke 19:5, 9

"On-Sight" Prayer

Read Acts 8:1-25, 9:32-42

I will give you every place where you set your foot.
Joshua 1:3

Marion, Indiana has the unfortunate brand as the location of the last lynching in the United States. A mere sixty years ago, two African American men were forced from their jail cells, taken across the street and hung in front of the county courthouse.

Not long ago, after conducting a prayer seminar in that city, we wrapped up our day by gathering downtown where that atrocity actually took place and holding a short prayer service. With us were two men: one older white man who had witnessed the lynching as a young boy, and another young black man who was a direct descendant of one of the victims. Together, the three of us poured oil on the pavement at the site, praying for forgiveness, healing and reconciliation. I believe we experienced a powerful spiritual breakthrough that would not have happened had we chosen to simply pray at the church.

Something stirs in us when we pray "on-site." When we move outside the four walls of our church and begin to pray on city streets, God gives us new "sight," and new vision for how to pray for people and places around us. When you go on the scene, different sights, smells and sounds will prompt you to pray in ways that you probably would never think of if you were to pray from a remote location. In their book, *Prayerwalking*, Hawthorne and Kendrick define this as "praying on site with insight."

"On-sight" prayer, which is what many simply call "prayerwalking," is an active strategy that calls Christians to identify targeted places or areas and then physically move about those premises to cover them in prayer. It is modeled in scripture by Abraham, who was a pioneer prayerwalker, and by Joshua. Jesus prepared His way through prayer, and the disciples prayed as they walked from city to city. God even made the promise to Joshua, "I will give you every place where you set your foot, as I promised Moses" (1:3). What a powerful principle to engage in our cities!

Of course, walking is not the only way to get on-site; you can sit, jog, bike, or do what I call "drive-by" praying; anything that will put you at the point of the need. For example, you could:

1. pray for each house on your block as you walk through your neighborhood;
2. sit in a hospital lobby and pray for the doctors, nurses, and patients;
3. jog around the high school track and pray for the students, teachers and administrators;
4. drive through a high crime area of your city and pray for peace;

Resource:

Prayerwalking
Steve Hawthorne and
Graham Kendrick

78

5. bike around a downtown area praying for the businesses and decision makers;
6. pray as you wait in a check-out line for the employees and other people in the store;
7. pray from a high point in your city—a hillside, a tall buildng—as you look out over the area;
8. walk through a crowded public place such as a shopping mall and pray for the salvation of all those who do not know Jesus.

I agree with Steve Hawthorne's observation that, "Some of our standard prayer meetings wobble between trivial matters of self-concern and topics of remote interest." However, he explains that people tend to pursue what they have prayed for and be involved with what they have seen. One of the advantages of "on-sight" prayer is that the experience can rejuvenate a passion for prayer because it stimulates a variety of avenues of intercession as you feel the pulse of your city. "Up close and personal prayer becomes an adventure; ...revealed insights often blend to fortify prayer with a starkly relevant authenticity," Steve says. As you pray "on-sight," God will give you His heart for the lost and hurting people around you, and He will show you needs and opportunities that you have never noticed before.

This kind of praying is already being done all over the country on a city-wide scale. For example, in Jackson, Tennessee, one lady enlisted hundreds of mothers to pray on-site at every public school in that city during the school year. In Austin, Texas, Steve Hawthorne's organization called PrayerWalk USA is currently working toward the vision of covering every ZIP code in America with "on-sight" prayer. And in Fayetteville, North Carolina, a group of Christians who were appalled by a race crime went to the police chief and obtained a map of their city outlining the areas where violent crimes happened most frequently. Then they formed teams and began to systematically cover those areas in prayer for reconciliation and peace. After two years, the overall crime rate in that city had declined an unprecedented 50%!

No longer will violence be heard in your land, nor ruin or destruction within your borders, but you will call your walls Salvation and your gates Praise.   Isaiah 60:18

For Group Discussion

1. Do you know of any "on-sight" prayer ministry going on in your church or city?

2. If you were going to pray for the emergency room, the firemen, city government, etc., how might being on the scene change the focus of your prayer?

3. Where is a good place to go and pray on-site for your entire city? List those who might go with you.

4. When is there opportunity in your normal routine for you to pray "on-sight"?

5. Write down three areas of your city that you feel called to pray for "on-sight." If you are in a group, share your response.

In Closing: Walk around your meeting place and practice "on-sight" prayer.

In prayerwalking, God is addressed and the city is blessed.   -Steve Hawthorne

Prayer Application
Week #6 - Praying on the Scene

DAY ONE
Read Joshua 1

Prayerwalk around your block asking God to fill each house with the love of the Lord.

Allow your spirit, as you pray, to be prompted by things you see such as toys in the yard, a wrecked car, beer bottles in the garage, a new baby sign, etc.

DAY TWO
Read Psalm 12:1-3

Pick, at random—a park bench, a coffee shop, a store—and pray for the people you see. Pray simple prayers like
> "Lord, reveal yourself to that woman and her two children."
> "Bless that man in Jesus' name."

DAY THREE
Think on Isaiah 53

Visit a courthouse and pray for what goes on there:
> Pray for wisdom for the Justices.
> Pray for a spirit of peace and tranquility in the courtrooms.
> Pray for supernatural healing of conflicts.
> Pray for comfort for those who have been victimized.
> Pray for true repentance and forgiveness to flow.

DAY FOUR
Read Isaiah 59:14-16

Drive by and pray for a school or day care center.

Ask God to reveal a way to reach the children and youth in your city.

DAY FIVE
Read Isaiah 29:13-14

Drive by or visit your local police station. Intercede for the officers' safety, alertness, effectiveness, judgment and character.

Get a list of the ten most wanted suspects in your area and pray for their capture.

DAY SIX
Read Psalm 69:30-34

Prayerwalk a local mall. Focus on praying for those who appear stressed or distressed.

Thank God for His provision, and entreat Him to bless the merchants and the financial economy in your city.

DAY SEVEN
Read Psalm 24:3-8

Pick a sister church and pray on-site for the pastoral staff.

Pray that they would be blessed with
      many conversions
      abundant finances

Personal Reflections and Answers to Prayer:

Notes

Guidelines for Neighborhood Prayerwalks

1. Go with a blessing from your pastor.
2. Recruit some partner prayerwalkers.
3. Limit the length of commitment.
4. Train the prayerwalkers.
5. Schedule prayerwalking times.
6. Form prayer teams.
7. Choose routes rather than following routines.
8. Debrief and report after each prayerwalk.

Taken from *Prayerwalking* by Steve Hawthorne and Graham Kendrick

Jesus looked at him and loved him.
Mark 10:21

Spontaneous Prayer

Model **#7**

Read Acts 8:26-40, 9:10-19

In Acts 8, after preaching the good news and baptizing many people in Samaria, Philip heard a strange word from the Lord—go stand on a road outside of town. God did not tell Philip why he was to "go south to the road," nor did He tell him what to do when he got there. He simply said, "Go." But that was not all. As Philip made his way on the road, he met a chariot, and the Spirit nudged him again to go "stay near it." I can just imagine Philip, wandering down this desert road trying to "act natural" as he worked to figure out how he might explain his presence to the chariot driver.

What Philip may or may not have realized, however, was that God was orchestrating a divine intersection. He was moving Philip in place in response to what I call an "open window."

After many years of pastoring and sharing the Gospel under all kinds of circumstances, I have come to the conclusion that every person has a kind of "spiritual window" through which they can receive the message of Jesus. At any given point in time, most people around us are so busy going about their routines that their windows are either shut or only partially open. Life is running smoothly enough that they are not inclined to want to hear what God has to offer them. Any attempts to witness may seem to bounce off and not be heard. But occasionally, someone gets knocked off center—some bad news, a disappointment, a loss, a heartbreak, confusion—and suddenly their window flies open as they search for meaning. At that point, they are a conversion waiting to happen.

Because Philip was in tune with God's voice and willing to obey His instruction, no matter how silly it may have seemed, the Ethiopian eunuch, who was a city leader, immediately accepted the message of the Gospel and was baptized! In the same manner, when Ananias obeyed God's leading to go to the house of Judas on Straight Street and lay hands on Saul, even though Saul had a reputation for arresting followers of Jesus, the result was the same. Saul was filled with the Holy Spirit and baptized. God directed Ananias to the open window.

Planning and scheduling prayer is important. But we must always bear in mind that God is constantly moving and working in the earth. His Spirit is brooding over your city even at this very moment in search of hearts that are open to receive Him. When a window of opportunity is revealed, God will use anyone who is listening for His voice to carry the message of His love through it. He will direct you to pray in His will and timing that a soul might be redeemed. He may ask you to do something you have never done before and will probably never do again, which is why we call this "spontaneous prayer."

Resources:

How to Listen to God
Charles Stanley

The Voice of God
Cindy Jacobs

"Holy Hunches"

This type of spontaneous prayer is dependent on hearing God. He must speak to us and we must hear and obey. But for many, hearing God seems difficult.

Jesus said that his sheep would hear His voice (John 10), but how does God speak? Although I know a couple of very godly men who have had experiences in which they heard God speak to them in an audible voice, for most of us, that is not the case. Most Christians "hear" God through what I call "holy hunches." As the Holy Spirit nudges, prompts and encourages, if we are in communion with God, we feel tugged or pulled in the direction He wants us to go. The Spirit has a way of bringing a person's name to mind or planting an idea in your head that just will not go away until you have obeyed what He is asking you to do. He speaks to your spirit.

The trouble is, we all have "hunches" all the time, probably several times every day. But not all of them are holy. You must evaluate what you hear and test it to know if it is from God. Peter Lord, in his book *Hearing God*, explains that God's voice will always be relevant; it will always deal with the matter at hand; it will always be pertinent; and it will always be applicable with regard to:

◆ Time—His word is now.
◆ Resources——He provides what He guides.
◆ Circumstances—He speaks in the midst of these.
◆ His Ways—He will not violate His self-established ways.

We can also know God's voice by:

◆ ...how it reflects His nature.
◆ ...how it relates to scripture.
◆ ...how it promotes salvation in the city.
◆ ...how it addresses the sins of the city.
◆ ...how it fosters unity in the corporate body of Christ.
◆ ...how it offers mercy and forgiveness.
◆ ...how it challenges and builds our faith.
◆ ...how it encourages the Church.

The Lord's voice will produce peace, hope, excitement, faith and praise. It will always stir us to actions that glorify the name of Jesus.

> *Imagine this...*
>
> *Going through life without hearing from God is like flying an airplane by sight. It works fine as long as the skies are clear. But when we learn to listen and hear His direction, then we are flying by instruments, and even the thickest fog and the darkest storm clouds can not keep us grounded.*

> *And yet when I say that the Lord has spoken to me, I mean something even more specific than general revelations or private inner impressions. I reserve these words intentionally for the rare, special occasions when, in my spirit, I have had the Lord speak directly to me. I do not mean, "I felt impressed," or, "I sensed somehow." Instead, I mean that at a given moment, almost always when I have least expected it, the Lord spoke **words** to me. Those words have been so distinct that I feel virtually able to say, "And I quote." -Jack Hayford*

For
Group
Discussion

1. Have you ever experienced a divine appointment similar to Philip's?

2. Looking back at the past week, was there a time when someone might have had an "open window"? Did you take the opportunity to pray or share?

3. Think of some times that you prayed spontaneously for people or situations. Did they all involve a crisis?

4. Do you hear from God? How do you recognize His voice?

5. What can you do to improve your hearing?

In Closing: Spend five minutes in silence and then give opportunity to share what the Lord spoke.

...All over the world this gospel is bearing fruit and growing, just as it has been doing among you since the day you heard it and understood God's grace in all truth.   Colossians 1:6

Prayer Application
Week #7 - Listening to God

DAY ONE

Read Acts 8:26-40, Acts 9:10-19

Write down a few things that God has spoken to you in your life.

Give thanks to Him for being a Father who cares and desires a relationship with you.

DAY TWO

Read II Chronicles 13

Be still and listen for at least 5 minutes to the Holy Spirit for a name or face to pray for.

Listen for a way to pray.

DAY THREE

Read I Timothy 2:1-8

Be quiet and listen for at least 10 minutes for a civic leader or government official for whom to pray.

Write a prayer to them based on Psalm 23.

DAY FOUR

Recite Luke 11:9-10

At an appropriate time today, tell a stranger that you meet that you are a Christian and ask if they have any special needs that you could pray for.

DAY FIVE

Read Romans 12:1-2

Ask God to speak to you about His will for your life, then listen quietly for at least 15 minutes to what He might say.

Pray for discernment.

DAY SIX

Read out loud Ephesians 3:14-21

Pray for God to fine tune your spiritual hearing.

Sit quietly for at least 20 minutes in His presence and meditate on His greatness, His faithfulness, His worthiness, His sacrifice, and on His majesty.

DAY SEVEN

Read Revelation 4

Write down a few of the things you heard God speaking to you this week. Also write down something you did that made it easier for you to listen.

Then the Lord called Samuel. Samuel answered, "Here I am." I Samuel 3:4

Personal Reflections and Answers to Prayer:

Notes

God shapes the world through prayer.
-E. M. Bounds

Prayer and Fasting
Read Acts 8:26-40, 9:10-19

What do Bill Bright, Martin Luther and John Wesley have in common with heroes and heroines of the faith such as Moses, David, Nehemiah, Esther, Daniel, Elijah, Hannah, Jesus, Paul, John, the disciples and Anna? In the lives of all of these men and women of God, fasting was or is an important part of their relationship to God and to their roles as Christian leaders.

Sometimes, when we begin to earnestly seek the Lord in a deeper way, we must be willing to have less of something "lesser." Whether we choose to fast food, a habit, or something else we deem significant, the sacrifice, if done in the right spirit, fosters in us a new and fresh humility and dependence on God. Today, many Christians of are rediscovering the power of fasting in conjunction with prayer as a fundamental discipline of the faith and as a means of achieving a spiritual breakthrough.

As I travel across America, I see cities running out of solutions. Our communities today can be so entangled in sin and wickedness that the answers lie beyond human means. Money can not be spent fast enough to solve escalating social problems. The needs of the poor overwhelm all of the humanitarian organizations in town. The churches are struggling just to maintain while the percent of those who are unchurched remains constant. Testimonies of healings, conversions and miraculous provision seem far apart and even non-existent. Discouraged pastors may feel that "the glory of God has departed" to another church or city.

It is at this point of desperation that many spiritual leaders are coming together to unite with each other in corporate fasts. Extreme circumstances call for drastic measures, motivating pastors to humble themselves and seek God for a new release of His Spirit. For example, in the Metroplex (the area between Dallas and Fort Worth), 180 pastors recently went on a forty day fast as they prayed for spiritual awakening to come to all of the churches in that area. Several pastors in Kansas City did the same. In November of 1996, in St. Louis, Missouri, 3,000 Christian leaders joined Bill Bright for a three day fast to pray for a breakthrough in our nation. The list goes on. The hunger for more of God is causing people to eliminate all distractions in order to gain a fresh focus on the person of Jesus Christ.

Resources:

Fasting for Spiritual Breakthrough
Elmer Towns

7 Basic Steps to Prayer and Fasting
Bill Bright

What Happens When We Fast?

Prayer and fasting...

1. ...helps us to hear from God. In Exodus 34:28, Moses fasted, heard from God, and then wrote the Ten Commandments.
2. ...is done when we sense an urgency in spiritual matters. In

I Kings 19:8, Elijah fasted because of the urgency of the moment.

3. ...can enable us to feel the burden of the Lord. In Ezra 10:6, Ezra prayed and fasted when he felt the heart of God.

4. ...helps to bring about spiritual breakthroughs. In Daniel 10:3, when Daniel was in a hard place, he got serious in prayer and fasting because he needed God to intervene in a mighty way.

5. ...helps us focus on what God wants. In Luke 4:1-2, Jesus fasted for focus at the start of His mission.

6. ...is sometimes needed for repentance and contrition over sin. In Acts 9:9, Paul fasted when he realized how wrong he had been.

7. ...is needed for consecration, or setting apart, for special ministry. The early church fasted and prayed when it elected and commissioned leaders (Acts 13:2-3, 14:23).

8. ...is good discipline for the Christian faith. Fasting denies the flesh to invite the Spirit (Rom. 13:14, Gal. 5:16, Col. 3:5).

9. ...breaks the yoke of bondage (Is. 58:6).

10. ...fosters healing and answers to prayer (Is. 58:8).

> *Imagine this...*
>
> *The pastor of Voice of Pentecost Church in San Francisco called his people to an interesting 40-day fast. In order to deal with a spirit of religion, he organized his entire congregation to hang door hangers of blessing on every home in the city instead of coming to services on Sunday mornings. At the end of the 40 days, he found that instead of losing members, as some had predicted he would, his church had actually grown in number.*

A Word of Warning

Like no other prayer model mentioned here, fasting seems to carry with it the danger of pride. Because there is something inherently noble about the idea of self-imposed sacrifice, it is easy for those who are fasting to desire recognition and admiration from men. In his book *What the Bible Says About Healthy Living*, Rex Russell, M. D. says this:

> Fasting is not a competitive sport. You do not have to set any records. Your body does not get healthier [*or more spiritual*] if you out-fast your friend or opponent. Don't sulk if your spouse "out-fasts" you. God does not give you more pleasure or a special crown for suffering more than anyone else. There is no scorecard! [Italics mine]

Check your motives. Seek God's direction about fasting. Do not be like the hypocrites who "disfigure their faces that they may appear to men to be fasting" (Matt. 6:16), but seek only the approval of the Lord.

> *There is no question that there is awesome power in fasting. If the fast is controlled by the Holy Spirit and Jesus is foremost, then it is a beautiful and powerful experience.*
> *-Arthur Blessitt*

For Group Discussion

1. Have you ever fasted?

2. Are you afraid of fasting? Why?

3. What are some of the common misconceptions that people have about fasting?

4. Read over the Prayer Application for this week. What do you think of the fasting exercises?

5. Why do the scriptures instruct us not to ring bells and blow whistles about our fasting? (Matthew 6:17,18)

In Closing: Repent of your lack of self-sacrifice for Kingdom agendas.

From the divine standpoint, it seems the Lord is especially willing to answer prayer when we put that prayer before our necessary food.   -William MacDonald

Prayer Application
Week #8 - Prayer and Fasting

DAY ONE
Read Isaiah 58

Ask God to help you fast for a spiritual breakthrough in some area of your life. Write down the breakthrough you need.

Fast the time you would normally watch TV today to seek God and pray for direction.

Then Jesus was led by the Spirit into the desert to be tested by the devil. After fasting forty days and forty nights, he was hungry. Matthew 4:1-2

DAY TWO
Read Isaiah 58

Fast one hour of sleep, either at night or in the morning, to read the Word.

Ask God to reveal sin in your life and repent of these things that grieve Him.

DAY THREE
Read Isaiah 58

Give up one meal and spend the time praying instead.

Beseech God to burden you with what burdens Him. Ask Him to give you a passion for the lost.

DAY FOUR
Read Isaiah 58

Pray for organizations in town that feed the poor or help those in need.

Send a check to one of these organizations for an amount that you would normally spend eating out.

DAY FIVE

Read Isaiah 58

Drink only water or juice until 3:00 p.m.

Beseech God for...
>   unity among the believers in your city.
>   salvation for a lost loved one.
>   a spiritual awakening in our nation.

DAY SIX

Read Isaiah 58

Make a list of the ways you are blessed simply because you live in this country.

Fast a negative thought or attitude that has been hindering you lately.

DAY SEVEN

Read Jeremiah 33:3

Call to the Lord and ask Him to show you a new way to please Him.

Sit quietly before God and listen to what He has to say to you. Ask Him to specifically show you areas in your life where fasting would please Him.

Jesus returned to Galilee in the power of the Spirit.... Luke 4:14

Personal Reflections and Answers to Prayer:

Seven Basic Steps to Successful Fasting

1. Set your objective. Why are you fasting?
2. Make your commitment with regard to duration and type of fast.
3. Prepare yourself spiritually. Begin with prayer and repentance.
4. Prepare yourself physically. Do not rush into the fast, and consult a doctor if necessary.
5. Put yourself on a schedule including praise, prayer, meditation and food or liquid intake.
6. End your fast gradually. Reintroduce solid foods and normal diet patterns slowly.
7. Expect results!

Adapted from *7 Basic Steps to Successful Fasting and Prayer* by Bill Bright

So we fasted and entreated our God for this, and He answered our prayer.   Ezra 8:23

"Pre-Prayer" for Worship Services

Read Acts 4:23-31, 13:1-3, 16:25-31

Model **#9**

True or False?

1. We can expect to have dynamic worship just by showing up at church.
2. People receive truth in a worship service if the speaker has a doctorate.
3. Music and praise is inspirational if the building is air-conditioned.
4. People will come to Christ if there is enough leg room to get out of their seat and go forward.
5. Ushers are the key to good attendance.
6. The Lord only inhabits the praises of those who raise their hands in church.
7. Moving the piano or inviting a guest soloist will destroy the spirit of worship.
8. If you can sing all the words without messing up, you will experience deep, personal worship.
9. Any move of the Spirit during the service is only permissible if it is printed in the bulletin.
10. Increasing the number of church social functions will automatically increase the number of baptisms each week.

A Welcome Mat

More than any other reason, people come to church because they need a touch from God. They want more of Him in their lives, maybe even in a particular area or situation. The goal of our worship, then, should be that every person present might experience His love and mercy in some manner, and that those who do not know Jesus would be drawn to Him.

But that kind of worship does not just happen; nor can it be produced simply by going through the motions. It must be inspired by the presence and working of the Holy Spirit, and the Spirit will come in answer to prayer.

If you were to research all of the fastest growing, most dynamic churches in the world where people are coming to Christ in large numbers on a regular basis, you would find one commonality: not a single worship service is held without a prayer force before, during and after. They mobilize people to pray for the services, pushing back the forces of darkness and inviting the Holy Spirit. This principle can be seen at work in the explosive Korean churches, as well as many in churches in this country.

96

"Pre-prayering" for worship can be done...

1. **During the week** - People can sign up to pray on an assigned day during the week for the services the following Sunday.
2. **On Saturday** - Prayer vigils can be scheduled on Saturday or the building can be opened Saturday night for people to walk through and pray over the pulpit, the chairs, etc.
3. **Early Sunday morning** - Some may be willing to come to the church early and simply sit and invite the Holy Spirit's presence.
4. **At the start of the service** - As the service begins, invite people to come kneel at the altar to pray for what is about to happen.
5. **During the service** - Enlist a team of intercessors to pray in another room while the service is going on.
6. **During the service** - Include time for prayer, other than by the pastor, in the order of worship. This could be done in small groups, at the altar, or in the seats.
7. **After the service** - Invite those who will to linger after the service and pray for the Spirit's work to be sealed in the hearts of those who were there.

Using the "'Pre-Prayer' for Worship" prayer card, invite the Holy Spirit to church with you. Welcome Him to:

◆ put in us a hunger for God's Word.
◆ reveal the Word to us.
◆ fill us with joy and delight in the Lord.
◆ make worship exciting and meaningful.
◆ touch us and heal us in worship.
◆ anoint the preaching and singing.
◆ lead us in worship to pray for other churches in the city.
◆ draw the unchurched to worship.

Imagine this...

One Sunday morning we had a "perfect" service. The music was inspiring, the testimony was moving, the offering was abundant, and the sermon was challenging. But as I left the church, feeling quite content and a bit proud, the Holy Spirit spoke to me, "The service was a failure." "What?" I thought. "Why?" The Spirit arrested me, "Because no one came to Christ."

*Charles Spurgeon had large groups of intercessors praying in a basement room **under** his pulpit in each service he preached. He called it his divine "furnace room."*

For
Group
Discussion

1. Is praying before the service a new idea at your church?

2. Think about your Sunday morning routine. When you sit down in the pew is your heart ready to receive God?

3. Would praying before the service increase your ability to receive from God?

4. Review the "Holy Spirit Factor" on page 16. In the spiritual realm, compare the difference between a prayed-for service and one that was not prayed for.

5. Is God always present in your service? Does He always act?

In Closing: Pray for your Sunday morning service this week.

Prayer is an engraved invitation for the Holy Spirit to come.

Prayer Application
Week #9 - Inviting the Lord to Worship

Read Psalm 63

Seek God for your pastor to receive the word of the Lord for your church this week.

Pray for him or her to have adequate preparation time and rich prayer time.

DAY TWO

Read Psalm 150

Lift up in prayer your music director and musicians. Ask God to bestow a special anointing on the selections, special presentations, etc. so that people might be drawn to receive Christ even during the praise time.

Pray against all possible obstacles to the best expression of worship.

DAY THREE

Read Philippians 4:19

Claim a rich blessing to be bestowed on God and for the name of Jesus to be lifted up during the worship service.

Pray for the offering to be beyond what is needed to meet the budget this week.

DAY FOUR

Read Acts 3

Go to the sanctuary and pray over each seat for the felt needs of the people to be met.

Kneel at your altar and envision many coming there on Sunday morning to repent (Acts 2:37).

DAY FIVE

Read Isaiah 43:5-7

Do a prayerwalk around your church building. Pause on each side, facing the north, south, west and east, and ask God to release the unchurched to be drawn to worship on Sunday morning.

Pray that your church sign will supernaturally draw needy people into the service.

Pray that many will be baptized this week and every week.

DAY SIX

Read Exodus 17:8-16

Organize a group of men and women to pray during each service on Sunday.

Ask your pastor for a copy of his or her sermon notes or text and for a list of desired responses so that the intercessors can pray in an informed manner.

DAY SEVEN

Read Psalm 150

Make a list of all the ways God has blessed your church.

Write down a prayer inviting the presence of the Lord into the services and send it to your pastor.

And the disciples were filled with joy and with the Holy Spirit. Acts 13:52

Personal Reflections and Answers to Prayer:

I urge, then, first of all, that requests, prayers, intercession and thanksgiving be made for everyone....   I Timothy 2:1

Warfare Prayer

Model **#10**

Read Acts 16:16-34

On Good Friday in 1988, I witnessed one of the most dramatic deliverances that I never thought possible. One of my church members was visibly set free from an oppression that caused uncontrollable anger in his life, and his personality underwent an immediate and complete transformation. So did my attitude toward spiritual warfare.

In the last ten years, much has been written in the area of spiritual warfare as the American Church has been learning what many third world churches have known for a long time—that our battle really is not against flesh and blood but against rulers, authorities and spiritual forces of evil in the heavenly realm (Eph. 6:12).

The kind of prayer that Paul employed in Acts 16 to drive the evil spirit out of the slave girl is what Richard Foster calls "authoritative prayer." He says:

> In authoritative prayer we are calling forth the will of the Father upon the earth. Here we are not so much speaking <u>to</u> God as speaking <u>for</u> God. We are not asking God to do something, rather, we are using the authority of God to command something done.

As believers, we have been given the power of attorney in Jesus' name to assert His finished work on the cross over the evil one. It is a prayer of eviction. Jesus often used authoritative prayer Himself, as when He told the wind and the waves to "be still," the lepers to "be clean," and the eyes of the blind to "be open." He commanded the paralytic to "get up," Lazarus to "come forth," and He ordered demonic spirits to "come out!" In Matthew 10:1, Jesus called his disciples to Himself "and gave them authority to drive out evil spirits" just as He had done.

Guidelines for Spiritual Warfare

1. ***Don't be trigger happy; not everything is an evil force.*** Spiritual warfare should only be done as a last resort; it is never a "quick fix" for a first encounter. Before you engage, study to gain understanding. Seek the wisdom of other godly men and women who have done it with good results.
2. ***Before you go after the rats, try taking out the garbage.*** Evil can only reside where there is sin, so do all you can to address the sin issues in your city. You may find that when you get rid of the garbage, the rats leave without an argument.
3. ***Make no kamikazi flights.*** Warfare is not meant to be a solo act; it demands a unified front. Prayers of eviction are best served

Be strong and courageous.
Joshua 1:6

Resources:

Warfare Prayer
Engaging the Enemy
Breaking Strongholds
Confronting the Powers
C. Peter Wagner

Discerning of Spirits
Exposing the Accusor of the Brethren
Francis Frangipane

under the covering of the city-wide church.

4. **Prepare with prayer and fasting** (John 9:29). This ensures that you go into battle under God's authority, not your own. The lower you can humble yourself, the greater your chances for victory since God's power is made perfect in our weakness.

5. **Be sensitive to God's leading about time and place.** Spiritual warfare is not designed to be public entertainment. It is real; it is serious, and it can be dangerous. Charging out into the street before the light turns green is a good way to get run over.

6. **Focus on Jesus, not the critters.** You do not need to spend an inordinate amount of time "binding" and "casting out" because the name of Jesus is omnipotent. The resurrection notorized the ultimate eviction notice that was served at Calvary. In other words, it is not necessary to jump up and down on a dead roach.

7. **Cover and seal the encounter with free-flowing praise.** The Lord inhabits the praises of His people, which is why praise that magnifies Jesus is so offensive to Satan. As the Holy Spirit comes in response to praise, His presence displaces evil.

8. **Never allow warfare to become an end in itself.** This is not a hobby or an extracurricular activity. The objective must <u>always</u> be to set captives free so that Jesus is glorified and His reign is established in lives and cities.

9. **Maintain an attitude of humility; God is in the driver's seat.** The Almighty Creator of the universe does not require your help to dismantle a stronghold. However, because He loves you, He will occasionally allow you to put your hands next to His on the steering wheel. To respond with arrogance or pride would be foolish.

10. **Keep in mind the "onion principle."** When you peel off one layer, you may find another underneath that looks just like it. Sin and evil often grow like an onion—you may peel away a crime problem and discover a deeper issue of racism. Behind the racism may be a layer of disunity. And beneath the disunity may be a hard core of pride. Go one step at a time.

> *Imagine this...*
> Our Western culture is hampered in understanding spiritual warfare because of our "enlightened, self-dependent mindset that says, "If you can not prove it scientifically, it does not exist." If you track on a world map the "hot spots" where Christianity is growing rapidly today, you will note that in each of those areas such as Korea, China, Guatemala, Nigeria, or Argentina, the people have an understanding of the spirit realm that is quite different from ours.*
>
> Ed Silvoso, paraphrase

> *Our prime objective, therefore, in intercession and spiritual warfare, is not the removal of the enemy, but the return of glory; the restoration of God's needed favor. When we encounter a spiritual stronghold, it is not a testimony to the presence of a big demon, but rather to the absence of the glory of God.*
>
> *-John Dawson*

For
Group
Discussion

1. Does spiritual warfare frighten you?

2. Why are the following factors so important in spiritual warfare: focus, spiritual maturity, humility?

3. Share a <u>positive</u> example of spiritual warfare that you have experienced or heard about.

4. Can you identify patterns of sin or destruction in your area.

5. What do you take with you into a spiritual battle? Discuss Ephesians 6.

In Closing: Repent of our ignorance and our fear of the spiritual realm.

Love worship, not warfare, but when necessary, go to war.
-Dutch Sheets

Prayer Application
Week #10 - "Taking Out the Garbage"

DAY ONE
Read I John 2:1-3

Examine your life for personal issues for which you need to repent.

If you have an unresolved conflict with another person, seek out their forgiveness today.

DAY TWO
Read Isaiah 55:7

Ask God to show you any sins or unpleasing habits that have been handed down through your family lines.

Ask for forgiveness on behalf of your forefathers, and pray for Him to remove that curse of sin from your family beginning with you.

DAY THREE
Read Psalm 51

Seek God for an awareness of any corporate sins in your church such as pride, isolationism, apathy, negative attitudes toward another church, pastor abuse, gossip...

Without pointing fingers, write out a short prayer of repentance for any of these sins that you have committed and send it to your pastor.

DAY FOUR
Read II Chronicles 7:14

If you do not already know, find out if their are sin issues that are dividing your denomination.

Repent of these issues, asking God to pour out His Spirit throughout your churches.

DAY FIVE
Read Acts 3:19

Lament the sins of your city, past and present. Consider political decisions that may have grieved the heart of God, racial issues, etc....

Pray for city officials. If you know of a particular sin in your city's past that needs healing, go to the site of the sin and anoint it with oil.

DAY SIX
Read Joel 2:13, II Corinthians 7:10

Confess the sins of our nation such as prayerlessness, idolatry, greed, immorality, vanity...

Bessech God for His mercy to be poured out upon America and for a return of godly principles in our government, schools and courts.

DAY SEVEN
Read Jeremiah 33:3

Ask the Holy Spirit to reveal to you new insights about the "heavenly realm." Write down one or two questions that you have about spiritual warfare and ask God to direct you to the answers.

Personal Reflections and Answers to Prayer:

Constructing a Simple Spiritual Map

1. Find a large city map that can be placed on a wall or some other easily accessible location.
2. Place a like-colored dot on the map for every church in the city. Watch for concentrations of churches, or areas void of local churches.
3. Place other colored dots on the map for elementary, middle and high schools. Also locate community colleges and universities.
4. Mark government buildings on the map.
5. Identify the locations of sources for demonic influence in your city (bars, dance clubs, porno shops, sexually-oriented bath houses, etc.).
6. Identify sources of gross spiritual deception such as New Age bookstores, Unitarian/Universalist churches, Mormon churches, Christian Science Reading Rooms, locations used for occult activities, spiritism, palm readers, etc.

Taken from *Loving Your City into the Kingdom* by Ted Haggard and Jack Hayford

Therefore submit to God. Resist the devil and he will flee from you.   James 4:7

Masterpiece Revival

When I was a little boy, I planted a bean. Every day I would dig it up to see if it was growing, and every day, it looked just as it had the day before. Nothing happened until finally my mother said, "Leave it alone." After several more days of painful waiting, I was rewarded by a small, green sprout poking through the dirt.

Taking a city for God requires time. It is a process, not an event. As you begin to pray, I believe you can expect to encounter five stages in the awakening process.

The Nesting Stage

When a chicken lays an egg, she does not roll it down the chicken coup saying, "Look! Look! I have another egg!" She does not run around talking about it or showing it off to the other chickens. She does not even busy herself with preparation for the new arrival. She simply sits on the egg.

So it is with anything good from God. We must take the vision and desire for awakening and begin to pray—quietly and patiently—until we see revival break forth. This is the time for soaking prayer, not frenzied activity.

This phase is the hardest because we may not see any changes or signs that our prayers are doing any good. But it is also the most important because as we pray in agreement for what God is going to perform, we are preparing the way for Him to move. Just as the disciples prayed continually in the Upper Room, waiting until they had been clothed with power from on high, we must pray with perseverance.

The Arresting Stage

Many churches reach this stage only to turn back. The problem is that the more we allow the presence of God into our midst, the more the light of His holiness begins to illuminate the dark areas of our lives in which we really do not want God to meddle. He arrests us in our sins— pride, prejudice, self-righteousness, pastor abuse, prayerlessness, lusts of the flesh, man-centered gospels, greed—and calls us to repentance. As Mario Murillo says in his book *Critical Mass*, "Before we can have a spiritual awakening, we must have a rude awakening."

The Cresting Stage

In this stage, strange things begin to happen that are not addressed in the denominational handbook. Revival almost always interrupts busi-

Resource:
Pray the Price
Terry Teykl

108

ness-as-usual routines. In fact, there is nothing tidy about a real move of God! As the winds of the Spirit stir things up, the first waves of revival may manifest themselves in ways that we are not accustomed to. We may have to welcome people into our church family who do not look or dress like us. We might be called to minister to someone who is homeless or dirty. Someone might bring a guitar into the service or move the organ or sing a different song. God may even violate our personal theology by making His presence known in a way that calls us out of our spiritual comfort zone and into new territory.

It is important in this stage to exercise both tolerance and temperance—tolerance for the experiences of others that may seem strange to us, and temperance that we do not allow our own manifestations to offend or confuse anyone around us. God has given us a sound mind and self-control (II Tim. 1:7), which means that our spirit is subject to our will. To say that we have no control over our behavior is not in line with the way the Holy Spirit works. Temperance and tolerance are the guard rails that keep us from going over the edge.

Imagine this...

A Church of God in Columbia, SC received a prophecy that revival in their church would "come from the river." One night as the pastor was praying in the prayer room, a homeless man knocked on the door looking for food. The pastor prayed for the man, and then fed him. That one single encounter catapulted that church into such a dynamic outreach to the homeless that they now have a service especially for them which averages 200 in attendance. Incidentally, many of the homeless men and women in Columbia live under a bridge down by the river.

Harvesting

At the core of spiritual awakening must be salvation—new converts being drawn into the saving knowledge of Jesus Christ for the first time. It is about harvest and nothing less. We are not just praying for some esoteric experience that will give us goosebumps and make us excited; emotion alone will never produce anything eternal. Our purpose is to see large numbers of people saved. We must keep in mind that spiritual awakening is not for our benefit as believers, but for the sake of furthering the Great Commission and advancing His Kingdom in this generation.

The experience of revival in a church is not an end in itself; it is ultimately to renew believers' zeal for bringing new babes into the Kingdom. However, revival in the church is essential because God will never put live chicks under a dead hen.

Sustaining

Our goal is not just to start an awakening, but to sustain it. As John Wesley said, "It is better to retain than simply gain!" When the church begins to come alive with new excitement, it is easy to get so busy meeting the demands of growth that we forget what brought it about. But it is critical that we continue to pray, and even pray more fervently so that God will continue to pour Himself out. I recently worked with two large churches, both in revival for several months, that called for forty days of prayer and fasting in response to God's goodness to them.

Rotate prayer models and recruit different people to pray at different times. The more God does, the more you need to pray.

Masterpiece Revival

For some years, I have made it a practice to regularly visit places where revival is happening just so I can see and hear first hand what the Holy Spirit is doing in different parts of the world. For example, several years ago, my wife and I visited a church in Buenos Aires, Argentina called Waves of Love and Peace that has been running thirteen services a day, seven days a week since that time! The Spirit is moving so strongly there that literally thousands of people walk to that building every day to receive something from God. About two years ago, I had a chance to visit the Toronto Vineyard that has been in revival now for several years and I saw people coming from all over the world to receive ministry and just be loved on. They start praying at the altar with people at about 9:00 p.m. and generally are not able to conclude until 3:00 or 4:00 in the morning. And just recently, while in Pensacola, Florida doing a prayer conference, I visited the Brownsville Assembly of God outpouring where people line up at the door hours ahead of time because the expectancy for God to move is so strong. I was touched by their sensitivity to people of all denominations and by their emphasis on repentance and holiness.

But there are many others that, although not as well publicized, are every bit as exciting and valid. As I criss-cross the United States, I frequently stumble upon local churches that have quietly been experiencing similar explosive growth and signs and wonders to that of the more "high profile" revival sites. The United Methodist Church in Canton, Pennsylvania, for example, has grown from 40 to 140 in one year. For a town that size, that is remarkable! When I preached there, 200 people came out of the surrounding hills to learn about prayer. Another revival site is in an old building in downtown Houston where an African-American church, St. John's United Methodist Church, has grown from eight to 2,500 in five years, and has developed a dynamic ministry to the homeless. Not only are they feeding several hundred street people three times a week, they are also in the process of building a special home/school to meet the needs of children with AIDS. South Tampa Christian Center in Florida is another "spiritual hot spot." They have over 160 outreach ministries, and are considered to be one of the fastest growing churches in America.

To go to any of these places with an open heart is to receive a blessing. They are lifting up Jesus with their music, ministering to those with needs through prayer, and seeing many people come to Christ. But they are all uniquely different. God is on the scene; the Holy Spirit is doing a work. But the expression of that work in the individual churches is true to each one's style of worship and corporate personality.

Photocopy or Masterpiece?

I sense a danger at these revival sites—not in how the Holy Spirit is manifesting Himself, or how financial offerings are being used, but in what I call "revival clonism." The danger lies in the attempt to copy or clone the spiritual phenomenon by retracing the steps that seemed to produce it.

Americans are copy-cats. We have that photocopy mentality that causes us to study the success of others and then try to recreate it to make it our own. We see something that is working and we mimic it. We see an idea we like and we steal it. Volumes have been written on how to succeed at everything from business to relationships based on the methods of others who have made it work in the past.

In and of itself, of course, imitation is not bad. It is one of the purest forms of learning that we know. The problem is, some things, such as original works of art, were never meant to be duplicated. Revivals, renewals, and awakenings are copy-righted in heaven and can not be used without the consent of the Father.

What God wants to create where you live is an original masterpiece, not just a carbon copy. Like an artist expresses himself on the canvas, the Master wants to paint in your city a beautiful expression of His heart that is fresh and unique. He does not need the palette from Toronto or Pensacola. Rather, He will dip His brush into the gifts, talents and resources of your churches and blend them with the character of your town to create new colors and shades of awakening. He will take as much time as He needs to get every brush stroke just right. The result will be a dynamic revelation of Jesus that has never been seen before.

What this process requires of you is a certain wisdom and patience in approaching your city. You will need to resist the temptation to compare yourself to others, but remain focused on the Creator. Just as the brush does not argue with the painter about which stroke should come next, you must be open and willing to be used in whatever way He sees fit. It is much harder to pray, wait and listen for the Lord's direction than it is to run here and there looking for a formula. But the fruit of patience will be a genuine, sweet move of the Holy Spirit.

Imagine this...

A young woman in my church was murdered by two brothers. About a year later, the mother of the two convicted killers, both then on death row, joined our church. When one of the brothers was executed, the mother asked me to perform the funeral, at which 37 people came to Christ. Displayed at the memorial service was an exquisite painting of the crucifixion which the young man had painted in the months prior to his execution.

We don't wait well. We're into microwaving; God, on the other hand, is usually into marinating.
-Dutch Sheets

Appendix A:

Prayer Cards

Acts 29

ACTS 29
Prayer Guide
"Pray at all times in the Spirit." Ephesians 6:18

DAY ONE - Acts 1:1-14
" And with that He breathed on them and said, 'Receive the Holy Spirit." John 20:22

BESEECH	Jesus to reveal the Kingdom of God to your church. Mk. 1:14-15; Acts 1:3
ASK	Jesus to fIll these ministries with the Holy Spirit. Lk. 11:9-13; Acts 1:8
ENTREAT	the Father to loosen a spirit of corporate prayer in your church. Matt. 21:13; Acts 1:14; 1 Thess. 5:17

DAY TWO - Acts 2
"And in the last days, God says, 'I will pour out my Spirit on all people.'" Acts 2:17

SUPPLICATE	the Holy Spirit to extol the wonders of God in your community. Lk. 10:21-22; Acts 2:11
PETITION	that Jesus be lifted up in your church's proclamation. Jn. 12:32; Acts 2:36; Col. 1:28
CLAIM	apostolic results of repentance and water baptisms. Mk. 16:15-20; Acts 2:37-38, 4:30
ENVISION	the multiplying of small groups in your church for fellowshipping, Bible study, and prayer. Acts 2:42; Heb. 10:25
INVITE	the Lord to add to your number daily those who are being saved. Acts 2:47, 4:4, 5:14, 6:7, 8:12, 9:31, 11:21, 12:24

DAY THREE - Acts 3:1-21
"Oh Lord, our Lord, how majestic is your name in all the earth!" Psalm 8:1

PRAY	in Jesus' name for the following sick people to be healed... Lk. 10:9; Acts 3:6
PRAISE	His name for signs and wonders in the following school systems... Jn. 14:12
LISTEN	for a manner to pray over your city government. 1 Tim. 2:1-4

DAY FOUR - Acts 4
"But the Lord is faithful, and He will strengthen and protect you from the evil one." 1Thessalonians 3:3

BIND	in Jesus' name the powers of darkness resisting the gospel. Matt. 18:18-19
REQUEST	boldness for your pastor and church leaders so as not to compromise their message. Acts 4:31
THANK	God for His power in giving our testimony to the resurrection of the Lord Jesus. Acts 4:33; Col. 1:29

DAY FIVE - Acts 8
"So there was much joy in that city." Acts 8:8

INTERCEDE	that the gospel will be preached where it has not been heard. Acts 8:4; Matt. 28:19
BLESS	the Lord for raising up the following "Phillips" to evangelize your city... Matt. 9:37-38; Acts 8:5-7
SEEK	God for leaders to be saved as with the Ethiopian leader. Acts 8:35; 2 Tim. 2:1-6
EXPECT	breakthroughs in low income housing projects and apartment units. Acts 19:20; 2 Tim. 4:5

DAY SIX - Acts 9:1-31
"...you must be born again." John 3:3

BELIEVE God for the following to have a "Damascus Road" experience... Acts 1:1-6; Jn. 16:7-11

RAISE up, Lord, disciples like Ananias and Barnabas for new converts. Acts 9:15, 27, 9:31

DAY SEVEN - Acts 10
"Because our gospel came to you not simply with words, but also with power, with the Holy Spirit and with deep conviction..." 1 Thessalonians 1:5

BOLDLY pray for an alignment between those ready to hear like Cornelius, with those ready to tell like Peter. Acts 10:2, 23

DILIGENTLY ask the Holy Spirit to draw new households to come to church. Matt. 2:21; Acts 10:44; Heb. 11:6

DAY EIGHT - Acts 12:1-17

EARNESTLY pray for the following ministry casualties to be restored to the church... Acts 12:5, 7; James 5:19-20

REBUKE in Jesus' name the oppression and persecution of suffering Christians in other nations. Col. 2:2-3; Phil. 1:12

DAY NINE - Acts 16:16-34
"Worship the Lord in the splendor of His holiness." 1 Chronicles 16:29

AGREE in prayer for excitement and renewal of worship and praise in your church. Ps. 85:6; Matt. 18:18

ANOINT the worship leaders, musicians, and choir to sing under the blessing of the Holy Spirit. Lk. 4:18-19

LOOSEN a spirit of conviction of sin and a desire for conversion in your worship services. Acts 16:30; Rom. 1:16

DAY TEN - Acts 28:1-10
"Therefore, my dear brothers, stand firm. Let nothing move you." 1 Corinthians 15:58

COVET in prayer a spirit of steadfastness to complete this ministry to the end. 1 Cor. 15:58; 1 Tim. 6:12

RESIST in Jesus' name attacks on your pastor and church leadership. Acts 20:28-31; 2 Tim. 4:17-18

BUILD a hedge of protection around your church finances. Job 1:10; Ps. 91:11; Eph. 6:10-20

ALLOW the Holy Spirit to turn satanic attacks to the glory of God. Acts 28:7-10; Phil. 1:12

"And the disciples were filled with joy and with the Holy Spirit." Acts 13:52

EXPECT all that you have prayed. Eph. 3:20
CONFESS the work of the Holy Spirit to glorify Jesus. Jn. 15:26
ENCOURAGE others to pray with you that "Acts 29" will be written in your city. Acts 1:14

"The Lord's hand was with them, and a great number of people believed and turned to the Lord." Acts 11:21

Hedging in the Pastor

HEDGING IN THE PASTOR

Ephesians 6:10-18
"Be strong in the Lord and the strength of his might." Eph. 6:10

MEDITATE	on the greatness of God in behalf of your pastor. Romans 8:28, 31, 37, 1 Peter 3:12
EXPOSE	the wiles of the devil. Ephesians 6:11-12
CLAIM	scriptural promises for your pastor's overall protection. Isaiah 54:14-17, Ps. 34:7, Ps. 91, Luke 10:19, 2 Cor. 10:3-4
PETITION	the Father to grant _____ a discerning spirit. 2 Corinthians 11:14, 1 John 4:1

THE PASTOR'S PRIVATE LIFE
"Stand, therefore, girded in truth." Eph. 6:14

REQUEST	that your shepherd's glory be solely in the cross. Galations 6:14
PRAY	for continued rest and renewal. Isaiah 40:27-31, Heb. 4:1-13 for holiness. 1 Peter 1:16
SEEK	for _____ a clear vision of the merits of Christ. Phil. 3:7-10 for godly contentment. 1 Timothy 6:6 for the love of God to be shed abroad in his/her heart. Rom. 5:5

THE PASTOR'S PERSONAL LIFE
"Stand,...having put on the breastplate of righteousness." Eph. 6:14

INTERCEDE	for your pastor's spouse and children. Psalm 91:9-12, Psalm 37:25
CANCEL	in Jesus' name all assignments against them. Matthew 16:19
REMOVE	by faith all obstacles to their total health and prosperity. Mark 11:23, Philippians 4:19

THE PASTOR'S PRAISE LIFE
"Stand,...having shod your feet with the equipment of the gospel of peace." Eph. 6:15

ASK	the Father to give your shepherd strong worship. Matthew 4:10
BIND	the spirits of fear, gloom, and negativity. John 14:1, Isaiah 61:3, 2 Timothy 1:6-7
LISTEN	for any other direction to pray. Ecclesiastes 5:1-2

THE PASTOR'S PRAYER LIFE
"Stand,...above all taking the shield of faith, with which you can quench all the flaming darts of the evil one." Eph. 6:16

QUENCH	darts of doubt through the power of the Holy Spirit. Mark 6:5-6
REBUKE	all distractions from _____'s devotional time. Mark 5:36
LOOSEN	the forces of heaven to aid your pastor in prayer. Mark 1:35 (private prayer) Acts 1:14 (corporate prayer)

THE PASTOR'S PROFESSIONAL LIFE
"Stand,...taking the helmet of salvation." Eph. 6:17

SHIELD   my pastor from the fear of men. Isaiah 11:1-3, Proverbs 19:23

BESTOW   on _____ favor in the cities and nations. Proverbs 18:16

on him/her support from local churches. Proverbs 11:4

ENTREAT   Jesus to give your leader an uncompromising truth. Proverbs 4:20-27

Jesus to give him/her wisdom in leadership. James 1:5

THE PASTOR'S PREACHING LIFE
"Stand,...with the sword of the spirit, which is the word of God." Eph. 6:17

BLESS   _____ with rich study time. Acts 6:4, 2 Timothy 2:15

GRANT   my pastor a bold proclamation of Jesus. Colossians 1:28

my pastor opportunities to impact whole areas for Christ. Colossians 4:3-4

ANOINT   my shepherd to minister the grace of God. Lk. 4:18, 1 Jn. 2:27

him/her for apostolic results. Acts 2:37

_____ for signs and wonders. Mark 16:20

my pastor to reveal truth. Matthew 16:17

THE PASTOR'S PERSEVERING LIFE
"Stand,...pray at all times in the spirit, with all prayer and supplication.
To that end keep alert with all perseverance...." Eph. 6:18

HONOR   my pastor with lasting fruit in the nations. Mal. 3:11, John 15:16

CONFESS   steadfastness over him/her. 1 Corinthians 15:58

bold vision for your spiritual leader. Isaiah 41:10

rest and times of refreshing for him/her. Heb. 4, Matt. 11:28

GIVE   thanks for his/her call and gifts. Colossians 1:3-5

SECURE   _____ in courage. Joshua 1

"Fight the good fight of faith."
1 Timothy 6:12

EXPECT   all that you have prayed.

STAND   behind the pastor's family, girding them consistently in prayer.

YIELD   to the Spirit for other areas of prayer and intercession.

AMEN

Most Wanted

MOST WANTED LIST

How To Pray For the Lost

ASK GOD — to give us a burden for lost people.   Rom. 9:1-3; 10:1

CLAIM LABORERS — for the harvest.   Matt. 9:38

SEEK GOD — for opportunities for our congregation to witness and invite people to the Lord or to church.   Col. 4:2-4

RECEIVE IN PRAISE — the promise of fruit.   Jn. 15:16

REPENT — of fear in witnessing and petition God for church-wide boldness in witnessing.   Eph. 6:17-20; Acts 4:31-32

BESEECH GOD — to give us power to win the lost.   Acts 1:8; Col. 1:28

BELIEVE GOD — for conviction of sin.   Acts 2:37-38

BIND IN JESUS' NAME — the force of doubt veiling their minds.   2 Cor. 3:14-16; 4:3-4

PRAY — for their hearts to be opened to believe.   Acts 16:14

THANK — the Holy Spirit for wooing them to the Father.   Jn. 6:44; 16:7-11

PRAISE HIM — for miracles to happen to bring people to Christ.   Acts 3; Jn. 14:12-13

INTERCEDE — for a support base of literature, tapes, Bibles, and money to win the lost.   Deut. 8:18; Acts 28:10

REMIND GOD — in humility of His desire to reward our faith with souls. Heb. 11:6

REQUEST — a city-wide vision for the harvest in our city.   Jn. 4:35

EXPECT — people to be touched by the Holy Spirit as we worship God. Acts 16:25

INVITE GOD — to change your life as a sign to the lost.   2 Cor. 5:17

ENTREAT JESUS — for church-wide agreement in soul winning.   Matt. 18:18-19

DESIRE OF GOD — a creativity to be given to our church to win the lost.   Ps. 37:4

TRUST GOD — for a shepherding spirit to disciple and care for the new converts.   Ps. 37:3; Ezek. 34

WORSHIP HIM — for integrity and honesty in evangelistic outreach.   Jn. 8:29

ANTICIPATE — in prayer a great reaping on Sunday from what we have sown. Gal. 6:7-10

Personal

PERSONAL PRAYER GUIDE
Philippians 4:4-9

1 *Rejoice in the Lord always....Rejoice! Phil. 4:4*

Consider His goodness. Ps. 34:8, 37:3, 119:68
Ponder His fatherhood. Jn. 5:17, 8:28, 10:30, 14:6,
        14:9, 14:28, Rom. 8:15
Sing His praises. Psalms
Praise the name of the Lord. Ps. 52:9

2 *The Lord is near. Phil. 4:5*

Wait in awe. Is. 30:18, 40:31
Listen to the Holy Spirit. Jn. 15:26
Be still. Ps. 37:7, 46:10

3 *Do not be anxious about anything, but in everything, by prayer and petition, with thanksgiving, present your requests to God. Phil. 4:6*

Cast your cares on Him. 1 Pet. 5:7, Phil. 4:19
Give thanks to the Lord. Ps. 100
Pray, petitioning the Lord accordingly. (Daily Prayer Focus)
Count your blessings and answers to prayer. Matt. 7:11

4 *And the peace of God, which transcends all understanding, will guard your hearts and minds in Christ Jesus. Phil. 4:7*

Receive His peace. Jn. 14:27
Consider His works. Ps. 8:3, 1 Sam. 12:24
Rebuke fear in Jesus' name. 1 Jn. 4:18

5 *Whatever is true, ...noble, ...right, ...pure, ...lovely, ...admirable—think about such things. Phil. 4:8*

Read His Word. Ps. 119
Claim His wisdom. (one chapter of Proverbs per day)
Declare His power. (one chapter of Acts per day)

*The grace of the Lord Jesus Christ
be with your spirit. Phil. 4:23*

DAILY PRAYER FOCUS
Philippians 4:20

Mon
family
Mark 5:19

Thank the Lord for working in your family.
Claim salvation for friends and family members.
Pray forgiveness and healing over past hurts or sins.
Intercede for your children.

Tue
unity
John 17:26

Pray John 17 over the churches in your city.
Ask God for racial healing.
Repent of any corporate sins in the city.
Glorify Jesus for breakthroughs in unity.

Wed
world
Matt. 28:19

Intercede for world missions and missionaries.
Repent of something in our nation that grieves God.
Lift up those involved in a recent world tragedy.
Beseech God for a cure for _____.

Thu
evangelism
Matt. 6:10

Ask God to give unbelievers a hunger to know Jesus.
Believe God to raise up evangelists and spark revival.
Name schools and businesses, claiming salvation.
Prayerwalk in your own neighborhood or workplace.

Fri
leader
1 Tim. 2:1-6

Petition God for wisdom for government leaders.
Pray blessing and protection over spiritual leaders.
Thank God for those in authority who honor Him.
Intercede for educational and judicial systems.

Sat
needs
Phil. 4:19

Bless the Lord for His faithfulness in your life.
Forgive those who have offended you.
Present your personal requests to God.
Sing a song of praise to Him.

Sun
church
Phil. 1:9-11

Invite the Holy Spirit to your church's worship services.
Ask God to bless the pastor's message.
Trust the Lord for professions of faith.
Praise Him for all those who labor in the harvest.

"Pre-Prayer" for Worship

"Preprayer" for Worship

"...early will I seek Thee" (Psalm 63:1).

Driving to church...
+ Pray for His arrival.
+ Implore the Lord to protect all who are coming to the service (Ps. 91).
+ Trust God to draw the unchurched to worship.

Seeing the sign...
+ Pray for it to attract those who need to be there (Jn. 6:44).
+ Request the Holy Spirit to perform signs and wonders as you praise (Mk. 16:17).

Parking the car...
+ Petition Him for corporate placement in His will (Rom. 12:1-2).
+ Ask the Spirit to put a hunger for God in the heart of each person as they arrive (Matt. 5:6).

Standing at the front door...
+ Expect an open door for Jesus' presence and for those who are hurting or have been rejected (Rev. 3:8).
+ Bless the Lord for angels to protect each entrance (Ps. 91:11).

Bowing in the foyer...
+ Anticipate that mercy and grace will meet all persons (Ps. 51:1).
+ Welcome the Holy Spirit to fill each worshipper (Acts 2).

Entering the sanctuary...
+ Praise Him for a spirit of peace to flow throughout the building (Jn. 14:27).
+ Believe God for the greater works that Jesus promised (Jn. 14:12).

Laying hands on each seat...
✝ <u>Invite</u> the Lord, in Jesus' name, to meet felt needs (Acts 3).
✝ <u>Intercede</u> for particular families to hear a specific word of hope, comfort, etc.

Kneeling at the altar...
✝ <u>Picture</u> many coming to repentance and to a new life in Christ (Acts 2:37).
✝ <u>Listen</u> for ways to pray for special things such as communion, baptisms, etc.

Pausing in the pulpit...
✝ <u>Beseech</u> the Lord to bless the pastor to preach with boldness and compassion (Acts 4:31).
✝ <u>Earnestly</u> pray that Jesus be seen (Jn. 12:21).

Looking at the altar table...
✝ <u>Thank</u> God for all His provisions and bless Him for an abundant offering today (Phil. 4:19).
✝ <u>Trust</u> Him for all His gifts to be manifested (I Pet. 4:10).

Sitting in the choir loft...
✝ <u>Lift up</u> the choir and musicians to lead in exalted worship (Ps. 34:1).

Walking down the aisle...
✝ <u>Entreat</u> the Lord to challenge the congregation to go forth to fulfill the Great Commission (Matt. 28:19).
✝ <u>Claim</u> laborers for the harvest (Matt. 9:38).

Be still in humble gratitude (Ps. 46:10; Eph. 3:20).

75 Ways to Promote Unity in Your City

1. On Sunday morning, pray for another church to receive God's blessing. Send a letter to the church stating the blessing.
2. Receive a love offering once a month for another church.
3. Provide funds for the pastor of a smaller church to attend a conference or seminar.
4. Provide money for a pastoral family other than your own to have a vacation they otherwise could not afford.
5. Conduct a series of concerts of prayer.
6. Buy a case of Ted Haggard's book, *Primary Purpose*, and give one to every church in town.
7. If you are a pastor, swap pulpits with other pastors.
8. Invite a pastor or leader from another church to share in your service about something exciting the Lord is doing in their church.
9. Invite a pastor or leader of a different denomination to lunch just to visit.
10. Foster a pastors' prayer group.
11. Establish a place of prayer in the community that could be prayed in 12-24 hours a day by people from different churches.
12. Encourage men in your church to participate in Promise Keepers events.
13. Conduct a School of Prayer for churches in your area.
14. Have an annual Thanksgiving service with area churches.
15. Ask area worship leaders to combine their talents and record a community praise tape.
16. Organize a door hanger ministry to reach every home in your city.
17. Host a community concert with a Christian artist.
18. Enlist several congregations to meet at a different church on the first Sunday night of each month and worship together in the style of that church.
19. If you are in a pastors' prayer group, invite the mayor or other civic leaders to be a part of it.

20. Host a civic leaders' prayer breakfast.
21. Organize various pastors in town to pray at city council meetings.
22. Create a 24-hour prayer room at a local hospital.
23. Draw up a "Declaration of Interdependence" and enlist as many churches as you can to sign it.
24. Have a prayer summit.
25. Have a community sunrise service on Easter in the Wal-Mart parking lot.
26. Organize a racial reconciliation banquet and use the proceeds to scholarship children for Vacation Bible School at the church of their choice.
27. Study *Experiencing God,* by Henry Blackaby, with another church.
28. Exchange Sunday School teachers with another church for one Sunday.
29. Work together to put on a community crusade.
30. Begin building cross-denominational Houses of Prayer in various neighborhoods.
31. Launch a corporate time of prayer and fasting for your city.
32. Do a combined youth mission trip.
33. Have several churches pool resources to feed the poor at holiday times.
34. Organize a city-wide food pantry to which all the churches contribute.
35. Participate in a March for Jesus.
36. Make your building available to new churches that need a place to meet.
37. Send a group of skilled workmen from your church to do repairs on another church building.
38. Be willing to "loan out" leaders in your church to small or new churches that do not have money to support large staffs.
39. Send intercessors to various church parking lots on Sunday morning to pray for their worship services.
40. Put a list of all the city's churches and pastors in the prayer room to be prayed for daily.
41. Do a community church newsletter to report on what God is doing in the city.
42. Paint a sign for a church that does not have one.
43. Buy supplies for a new church.
44. Send your youth group to paint or clean a church of a different denomination.
45. Have churches pool resources to rent a billboard that advertises Jesus.
46. Meet regularly with the police chief or sheriff to get prayer requests.
47. Assign names of police officers, firemen, city workers, etc. to various churches to be prayed over daily or weekly.
48. Assign every public school to at least one youth group in town to pray for each week.
49. Start a community Moms in Touch group to intercede for teachers.
50. Set up a ministry network so that each participating church could focus on one ministry that it is called to. Each church would "tithe" to the others to support the ministries, and would refer people accordingly. For example, one church would have an outreach for unwed mothers, one would distribute clothing, while another might run an adult literacy program.
51. Distribute the *Jesus* video to each home in the city. Attach a note that reads, "From the Church of 'Smithtown, USA.'"
52. Distribute Bibles in the same manner, funded by all the churches.
53. Organize multi-denominational prayerwalks.
54. Make a commitment not to speak negatively about other churches.
55. Establish a sign, such as a candle in the window, for Christians to display in their homes as a reminder to pray for revival.

56. Encourage your church to hire staff members of other races.
57. Pool volunteers to do community projects together.
58. Recommend other churches to first time visitors.
59. Ask a Catholic priest to bless your church.
60. Rotate a cell phone prayer line among the churches.
61. Set up an inter-church prayer chain.
62. Invite other churches to your own church events.
63. Support a community missions outreach to the homeless.
64. Appoint a city-wide prayer coordinator to promote prayer and unity.
65. Do a joint revival using local pastors.
66. Do a feature story in your church newsletter on a church not like yours. For example, if you are a mainline church, do a story on a charismatic church.
67. Conduct a city-wide Solemn Assembly to repent of corporate sins.
68. Invite the Power Team to witness to the youth in the city. Hold the event in a public auditorium instead of your church.
69. Host quality seminars on worship, marriage, prayer, etc. and give discounts to people who are *not* members of your church.
70. Loan members to help start a new church.
71. If you are a pastor, preach a series of sermons on the strengths of other denominations and the importance of unity in the body of Christ.
72. Formally commission and bless members who leave your church to go to a different one.
73. Send money to other churches' missionaries.
74. Sing the songs of another church.
75. Create an area-wide prayer map and distribute copies to all the churches in town.

Now to the King eternal,
immortal, invisible, the only God,
be honor and glory for ever and ever. Amen.
I Timothy 1:17